13th Workshop on Building and Using Comparable Corpora (BUCC 2020)

Marseille, France
11 – 16 May 2020

Editors:

Reinhard Rapp   **Serge Sharoff**
Pierre Zweigenbaum

ISBN: 978-1-7138-1254-8

LREC 2020 Workshop
Language Resources and Evaluation Conference
11–16 May 2020

13th Workshop on Building and Using Comparable Corpora

PROCEEDINGS

Reinhard Rapp, Pierre Zweigenbaum, Serge Sharoff (eds.)

Proceedings of the LREC 2020
13th Workshop on Building and Using Comparable Corpora

Edited by: Reinhard Rapp, Pierre Zweigenbaum, Serge Sharoff

For more information:
European Language Resources Association (ELRA)
9 rue des Cordelières
75013, Paris
France
http://www.elra.info
Email: lrec@elda.org

Preface – 13th BUCC at LREC 2020

In the language engineering and the linguistics communities, research on comparable corpora has been motivated by two main reasons. In language engineering, on the one hand, it is primarily motivated by the need to use comparable corpora as training data for statistical Natural Language Processing applications such as statistical machine translation or cross-lingual retrieval. In linguistics, on the other hand, comparable corpora are of interest in themselves by making possible inter-linguistic discoveries and comparisons. It is generally accepted in both communities that comparable corpora are documents in one or several languages that are comparable in content and form in various degrees and dimensions. We believe that the linguistic definitions and observations related to comparable corpora can improve methods to mine such corpora for applications of statistical NLP. As such, it is of great interest to bring together builders and users of such corpora.

Comparable corpora are collections of documents that are comparable in content and form in various degrees and dimensions. This definition includes many types of parallel and non-parallel multilingual corpora, but also sets of monolingual corpora that are used for comparative purposes. Research on comparable corpora is active but used to be scattered among many workshops and conferences. The workshop series on "Building and Using Comparable Corpora" (BUCC) aims at promoting progress in this exciting emerging field by bundling its research, thereby making it more visible and giving it a better platform.

Following the twelve previous editions of the workshop which took place in Africa (LREC'08 in Marrakech), America (ACL'11 in Portland and ACL'17 in Vancouver), Asia (ACL-IJCNLP'09 in Singapore, ACL-IJCNLP'15 in Beijing, LREC'18 in Miyazaki, Japan), Europe (LREC'10 in Malta, ACL'13 in Sofia, LREC'14 in Reykjavik, LREC'16 in Portoroz, RANLP'19 in Varna) and also on the border between Asia and Europe (LREC'12 in Istanbul), this year the 13th edition of the BUCC workshop was supposed to be held in Marseille.

However, due to the corona crisis, unfortunately LREC 2020 could not be held in Marseille this year. Therefore, with full support of the LREC organizers, we decided to hold the BUCC workshop as a free online event on the planned date. This not only causes problems, but also offers chances which we are eager to explore. Fortunately, the fourth BUCC shared task on "Bilingual Dictionary Induction from Comparable Corpora" was not strongly affected by this change and could be successfully conducted with surprisingly good results. Several papers by the shared task participants in this volume as well as an overview paper provide more information on this.

We would like to thank all people who in one way or another helped in making this workshop once again a success. We are especially grateful to Khalid Choukri for his excellent and almost magical guidance concerning the proceedings, to Nicoletta Calzolari for her continuous support of our workshop, and to Hélène Mazo, Sara Goggi and the whole team of LREC organisers for finding solutions to all matters of concern.

Our special thanks go to Holger Schwenk and Jörg Tiedemann for accepting to give invited presentations and to the members of the programme committee who did an excellent job in reviewing the submitted papers under strict time constraints. Last but not least we would like to thank our authors, shared task teams and all participants of the workshop.

Reinhard Rapp, Pierre Zweigenbaum, Serge Sharoff   May 2020

Workshop Organizers:

Reinhard Rapp, Athena R.C., Magdeburg-Stendal University of Applied Sciences, University of Mainz (Chair)
Pierre Zweigenbaum, LIMSI, CNRS, Université Paris-Saclay
Serge Sharoff, University of Leeds

Programme Committee:

Ahmet Aker (University of Sheffield, UK)
Ebrahim Ansari (Institute for Advanced Studies in Basic Sciences, Iran)
Hervé Déjean (Naver Labs Europe, Grenoble, France)
Thierry Etchegoyhen (VicomTech, Spain)
Silvia Hansen-Schirra (University of Mainz, Germany)
Hitoshi Isahara (Toyohashi University of Technology, Japan)
Kyo Kageura (The University of Tokyo, Japan)
Yves Lepage (Waseda University, Japan)
Shervin Malmasi (Harvard Medical School, Boston, MA, USA)
Michael Mohler (Language Computer Corp., USA)
Emmanuel Morin (Université de Nantes, France)
Dragos Stefan Munteanu (Language Weaver, Inc., USA)
Ted Pedersen (University of Minnesota, Duluth, US)
Reinhard Rapp (Athena R.C., Magdeburg-Stendal University of Applied Sciences, University of Mainz)
Serge Sharoff (University of Leeds, UK)
Michel Simard (National Research Council Canada)
Richard Sproat (OGI School of Science & Technology, USA)
Pierre Zweigenbaum (Université Paris-Saclay, CNRS, LIMSI, Orsay, France)

Invited Speakers:

Holger Schwenk, Facebook Artificial Intelligence Research
Jörg Tiedemann, University of Helsinki

Table of Contents

BUCC 2020 Workshop Programme

Monday, May 11, 2020

Times refer to Central European Summer Time (UTC + 2)
https://www.timeanddate.com/worldclock/france/marseille

09:15–9:30   *Opening*

Session 1: Invited Presentation

09:30–10:20   Holger Schwenk, Facebook AI Research

Session 2: Shared Task: Bilingual Dictionary Induction from Comparable Corpora

10:20–10:40   *Overview of the Fourth BUCC Shared Task: Bilingual Dictionary Induction from Comparable Corpora*
Reinhard Rapp, Pierre Zweigenbaum and Serge Sharoff

10:40–11:00   *TALN/LS2N Participation at the BUCC Shared Task: Bilingual Dictionary Induction from Comparable Corpora*
Martin Laville, Amir Hazem and Emmanuel Morin

11:00–11:20   *Coffee Break*

11:20–11:40   *LMU Bilingual Dictionary Induction System with Word Surface Similarity Scores for BUCC 2020*
Silvia Severini, Viktor Hangya, Alexander Fraser and Hinrich Schütze

11:40–12:00   *BUCC2020: Bilingual Dictionary Induction using Cross-lingual Embedding*
Sanjanasri JP, Vijay Krishna Menon and Soman KP

12:00–13:00   *Lunch Break*

Session 3: Invited Presentation

13:00–13:50   Jörg Tiedemann, University of Helsinki

Session 4: Corpus Construction

13:50–14:10   *Constructing a Bilingual Corpus of Parallel Tweets*
Hamdy Mubarak, Sabit Hassan and Ahmed Abdelali

14:10–14:30   *cEnTam: Creation and Validation of a New English-Tamil Bilingual Corpus*
Sanjanasri JP, Premjith B, Vijay Krishna Menon and Soman KP

14:30–14:50   *Coffee Break*

Proceedings of the 13th Workshop on Building and Using Comparable Corpora, pages 1–5
Language Resources and Evaluation Conference (LREC 2020), Marseille, 11–16 May 2020
ⓒ European Language Resources Association (ELRA), licensed under CC-BY-NC

Line-a-line: A Tool for Annotating Word-Alignments

Maria Skeppstedt, Magnus Ahltorp, Gunnar Eriksson, Rickard Domeij
The Language Council of Sweden, The Institute for Language and Folklore
Box 20057, 104 60 Stockholm, Sweden
firstname.lastname@isof.se

Abstract

We here describe *line-a-line*, a web-based tool for manual annotation of word-alignments in sentence-aligned parallel corpora. The graphical user interface, which builds on a design template from the Jigsaw system for investigative analysis, displays the words from each sentence pair that is to be annotated as elements in two vertical lists. An alignment between two words is annotated by drag-and-drop, i.e. by dragging an element from the left-hand list and dropping it on an element in the right-hand list. The tool indicates that two words are aligned by lines that connect them and by highlighting associated words when the mouse is hovered over them. Line-a-line uses the efmaral library for producing pre-annotated alignments, on which the user can base the manual annotation. The tool is mainly planned to be used on moderately under-resourced languages, for which resources in the form of parallel corpora are scarce. The automatic word-alignment functionality therefore also incorporates information derived from non-parallel resources, in the form of pre-trained multilingual word embeddings from the MUSE library.

Keywords: Word-alignments, parallel corpora, annotation tools, multilingual word embeddings

1. Introduction

Word-aligned parallel corpora form useful resources for several tasks, e.g. for bilingual dictionary construction (Bourgonje et al., 2018), for studies of language typology (Dahl and Wälchli, 2016), for translation studies (Merkel et al., 2003), as well as for those types of machine translation systems that use word-aligned corpora as an intermediate step (Alkhouli et al., 2016).

For constructing alignment gold standards, e.g. for evaluating the performance of automatic word-aligners, there is a need for tools by which manual annotations of word-alignments can be performed. There exist many such word-alignment annotation tools, but these tools are typically either (i) several years old (Merkel et al., 2003; Zhang et al., 2008; Hung-Ngo and Winiwarter, 2012), or (ii) not targeting the core task of word-alignment of sentences belonging to two different languages (Wirén et al., 2018).

Annotation tools whose interfaces are not being modernised according to the possibilities offered by more recent graphical user interface libraries might, however, be perceived as not adhering to current graphical user interface conventions. This might in turn decrease the usability of, and trust in, these older tools, also when they offer a functionality that objectively should be adequate for performing the manual alignment annotations.

As an alternative to these older tools, we have used current libraries for web development for constructing an annotation tool to use for the task of word-alignment in sentence-aligned texts. With the aim of increasing the usability of the tool, we have used a design template from the field of visualisation research as an inspiration for the user interface design. To further facilitate the annotation, a selectable pre-annotation in the form of an automatic word-alignment is provided, on which the user can base their manual annotation.

We plan to use word-aligned corpora for performing translation studies, including research on the application of official terminologies in translated texts (Dahlberg, 2017).

We will particularly focus on moderately under-resourced languages and under-resourced language pairs, for which small monolingual corpora exist and only very small parallel corpora. The line-a-line tool therefore allows the user to choose between several methods for the pre-annotations of the word-alignments, i.e. the user can select the alignment method that is found most useful for the language pair targeted.

2. Previous tools

The following four tools form examples of tools developed for word-alignment between sentence-aligned parallel texts, or for related tasks.

The I*Link tool (Merkel et al., 2003) for word-alignment annotation proposes alignment candidates, using bilingual resources and built-in heuristics, and the user can then accept, revise or reject these proposals. The tool also saves the user's alignment choices and adapts new alignment suggestions to previous choices made. The sentence pair is displayed in two horisontal rows, and the colour in which the words are written is used for indicating which words that are aligned, i.e. aligned words are displayed with the same, unique colour.

Zhang et al. (2008) developed a word-alignment annotation tool targeted towards Japanese-Chinese parallel corpora. The sentence pairs are provided with pre-alignments through the GIZA++ word-alignment tool. The sentence pair is displayed in two horizontal rows, and alignments are indicated through connecting lines. The user can optionally create chunks of tokens in the individual languages, and align chunks instead of words.

The tool by Hung-Ngo and Winiwarter (2012) also displays the sentence pair in two horizontal rows, and uses connecting lines to show alignments. The sentences are pre-annotated through the use of bilingual dictionaries, and parse trees for the two sentences are also generated and displayed. Annotation is carried out through drag-and-drop of nodes that symbolise the words or other levels in the parse

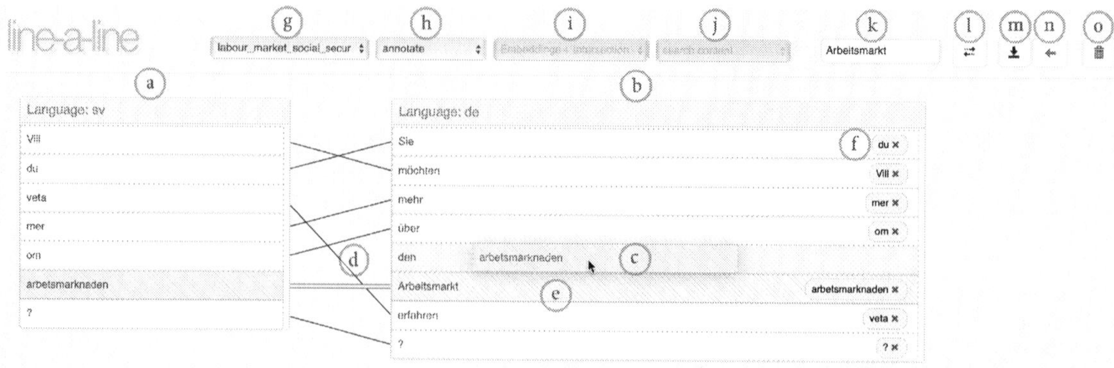

Figure 1: The user interface, showing a Swedish-German sentence pair. The following selections have been made by the user: (i) Annotation mode (**h**), (ii) to let the tool provide pre-annotated alignments through a union of intersection-symmetrising and the alignments produced during the dictionary creation (**i**), (iii) to select what to annotate through searching for word in the corpus (**j** - **k**). An alignment between two words is annotated through dragging the element from the left-hand list and dropping it on an element on the right-hand list. The figure shows how the user is dragging the element representing *'arbetsmarknaden'* with the aim of dropping it on the *'den'* element. When the user has dropped the element, an alignment between these two words will have been created.

tree. The tool also provides a visualisation of alignments in a matrix format.

The SVALA tool is constructed using current libraries for web development. Its purpose is, however, not to align sentences written in two different languages, but to correct and annotate text written by second-language learners. While the user is correcting the text, the tool maintains an automatic word-alignment between the original text and the corrected version. When necessary, it is also possible to manually correct the automatic word-alignments provided. Also this tool displays the sentence pairs in two horizontal rows, with connecting lines that indicate alignments.

3. The implemented word-alignment annotation tool

The line-a-line tool consists of a web-based front-end written in JavaScript/D3, and a back-end based on Python/Flask, a PyMongo database, as well as on the efmaral library (Östling and Tiedemann, 2016) for producing the automatic word-alignments used for the pre-annotations. Apart from being provided with the information available in the parallel texts, the automatic word-alignment functionality is also provided with data derived from a multilingual embedding space.

During the development of the tool, we used 559 sentence pairs from automatically sentence-aligned Swedish-German parallel texts, which have been collected from translations of Swedish government agency texts (Dahlberg and Domeij, 2017). We also used the Swedish-German multilingual embedding space available from the MUSE library.

3.1. Front-end

The interface for carrying out a manual word alignment is shown in Figure 1. The figure shows the tool applied to the corpus used during the tool development, with the Swedish text to the left and the German text to the right.

The interface contains the following components: (**a**) The sentence belonging to one of the languages. (**b**) The sentence belonging to the other language. (**c**) An alignment between two words is created by drag-and-drop, i.e. by dragging an element from the left-hand list and dropping it on an element in the right-hand list. (**d**) Alignments are shown by lines that connect the associated list elements. (**e**) In addition, when the user hovers the mouse over an element, its associated elements, and the lines indicating the association, are highlighted. (**f**) An alignment is removed by clicking on the corresponding delete button. (**g**) Drop-down list for choosing which corpus to annotate. (**h**) Drop-down for choosing either annotation mode or to browse previously annotated sentences in read-only mode. (**i**) Drop-down list for choosing which word-alignment method to use for the pre-annotation. There are three different word-alignments to choose from (see section 3.3. below), and the user can also choose to annotate the alignments from scratch without any pre-annotations. (**j**) Drop-down list for choosing the criterium by which the next sentence pair to annotate is to be selected. The user can choose the order in which the sentence pairs are to be annotated, i.e. to choose to start with the ones that the pre-alignment system estimates to be easiest or estimates to be most difficult, or to annotate the sentence pairs in the order in which they appear in the corpus. The user can also choose to annotate sentence pairs that contain a specific word, and the word to search for is specified in the text field (**k**). (**l**) Reverse the order in which sentences belonging to the two languages are displayed. That is, the German text would in this case be displayed to the left and the Swedish text to the right, if the order were reversed. (**m**) Save the alignment annotation. (**n**) Redo, i.e. go back to the previously annotated sentence pair. (**o**) Remove the sentence pair from the annotation task (e.g. when the sentence pair stems from an incorrect sentence alignment).

To be able to choose a sentence-aligned corpus for manual annotation – in the drop-down list (**g**) above – the Python script provided for loading it into line-a-line's database must have been executed. The sentence-aligned corpus must be provided in the Translation Memory eXchange (TMX) format. The loading script tokenises the sentences using NLTK's TweetTokenizer[1] (Bird, 2002), and saves the tokenised sentence pairs in the PyMongo database.

The user interface builds on a design template from a system constructed within the field of information visualisation research; the Jigsaw system for investigative analysis (Stasko, 2008). The Jigsaw system includes a list view user interface for visualising connections between different types of entities (e.g. people, places, dates and organisations) that are mentioned in a text collection. The interface displays each type of entity in separate lists, and associations between entities in the different lists are indicated by highlighting the entities and the lines that connect them. The same design template has also been used for visualising associations between information entities extracted from large text collections by the use of topic modelling (Skeppstedt et al., 2018).

Lists of words that form sentences in two different languages, and where some of the word-pairs in these two lists are connected, form a data set that is similar to the connected entity data of Jigsaw's list view interface. We therefore found the list view template suitable for the word-alignment task, where alignments are indicated by connecting lines and by highlighting of associated words and of lines that connect these words (shown in Figure 1).

To display the two paired sentences in the form of two vertical lists differs from the approach used in the systems mentioned above, which either display word-alignments through lines between two horizontal sentences, or in a matrix format. By instead arranging the words vertically, as we have done here, the display of the word associations becomes more compact for most writing systems, which has the potential to make it easier to trace the connecting lines. While this vertical view potentially de-emphasises the sentence, it instead emphasises the individual tokens, which might make it easier to focus on the parts of the sentences that are relevant for the immediate alignment connections that are created or inspected by the annotator.

3.2. An automatically created dictionary from multilingual word embeddings

As stated above, we plan to apply the tool on pairs of texts in moderately under-resourced languages, for which parallel resources are scarce. To improve the pre-annotation for these languages, information from monolingual resources should also be included in the automatic word-alignment functionality. To achieve this, the tool uses pre-trained multilingual embeddings from the MUSE library.[2]

By using the MUSE library, multilingual word embeddings can be constructed from independent monolingual resources. A multilingual word embedding is constructed from two separate monolingual word embedding spaces for the two languages in question. That is, each one of the embedding spaces is trained independently on a monolingual corpus. The embeddings for the two monolingual spaces constructed are then automatically aligned, i.e. pairs of corresponding embedding vectors are found in the two spaces. If there is a bilingual dictionary available, the alignment can be carried out in a supervised fashion. A subset of the embeddings can then be aligned with the use of the dictionary, and the alignments of other embeddings can thereafter be adapted to these points. The process can also be carried out in an unsupervised fashion without a dictionary, using a similarity measure called 'cross-domain similarity local scaling' for finding alignments between embeddings (Conneau et al., 2017).

The resulting multilingual word embedding space can then be queried for a word in one of the languages, which results in an output in the form of a list of the nearest neighbours to this word in the other language. We use this functionality to automatically generate a corpus-specific bilingual dictionary, which we give as an extra parallel data input to the word-alignment functionality described below. The method used for incorporating the embeddings is somewhat inspired by the work by Pourdamghani et al. (2018). They, however, use similarity in two monolingual spaces for inferring word-alignments.

The automatic creation of the corpus-specific bilingual dictionary is carried out as follows: For each sentence pair in the parallel corpus, i.e. the pair of two vectors of words, one belonging to language **a** and the other to language **b**, the following is carried out. All possible tuples consisting of one word from the sentence belonging to language **a** and one word from the sentence belonging to language **b** are constructed. For each such tuple (a_i, b_j), the multilingual word embedding space is used to check whether a_i is included among the top n nearest neighbours to b_j and whether b_i is included among the top n nearest neighbours to a_j. If both conditions are fulfilled, the tuple is added to the automatically constructed bilingual dictionary. The detected tuple is also recorded as a word-alignment for this specific sentence-pair, and this alignment is later used as a component in one of the pre-alignment options provided by the tool.[3]

If no match is found for any of the words in a sentence, we also allow for a search on subwords in the embedding space. Thereby, some morphological variations and compound words that are present in the sentences that are to be aligned, but not included in the embedding space, can be included.[4]

---

^[1]https://www.nltk.org/api/nltk.tokenize.html. The use of tokeniser will later be made configurable, as there are many languages for which the TweetTokenizer it is not suitable. For instance, Japanese and Chinese, which do not use white space to indicate token segmentation.

^[2]https://github.com/facebookresearch/MUSE

^[3]When developing the system we used $n = 2$, and if no match was found for a word, we allowed for an $n = 20$ for a word pair to be included in the dictionary. The cut-off used should, however, be allowed to be adjusted by the user. Punctuation characters and stop words are excluded from the dictionary construction process.

^[4]We here used a minimum allowed length of 4 characters for a

The word-alignments and the automatically created dictionary are then used as components for producing pre-annotated word-alignments.

3.3. Back-end with pre-annotated word-alignments

The corpus loading script also runs an automatic word-alignment, which is used for the pre-annotated alignments on which the user bases their manual annotations. The main method for producing the automatic word-alignments is the efmaral system (Östling and Tiedemann, 2016; Tiedemann et al., 2016)[5]. The efmaral system uses a Bayesian model with Markov Chain Monte Carlo (MCMC) inference for producing the word-alignments. The corpus-specific dictionary, automatically produced through the MUSE library, is used as additional input, i.e. as aligned data, for the efmaral word-alignment.

The efmaral alignment is run twice, first with one of the languages as source language and the other as target language, and thereafter with reversed language order. Three different methods are then available for symmetrising the alignments, (i) a simple intersection of the two alignment predictions, i.e. only keeping the alignments that are predicted by both models, or (ii) symmetrising using the GDFA word-alignment symmetrisation algorithm as implemented in NLTK[6] (Axelrod et al., 2005), (iii) a union of the intersection-symmetrising alignments and the alignments produced during the dictionary creation. The user can thereby choose the type of pre-annotation that is found most useful for the corpus that is being annotated. The user can also choose to carry out the annotation without using a pre-annotation of the alignments, as it is likely that there are circumstances when the pre-annotations would not be found useful. For instance, when the tool is applied on languages with very few existing resources, which would render low quality pre-annotations. None of the methods provided for pre-alignment rely on the existence of heavy resource-demanding language models, e.g., BERT models, as such models would be unobtainable for the low resource language pairs that form the target of the tool.

A difficulty score is computed for the alignments, by measuring the number of word pairs that are included in the intersection set in relation to the total number of words in the two sentences. This difficulty score is used for sorting the sentence pairs that are given to the user for manual alignment. Depending on the choice made by the user in the drop-down list (**i**), the back-end either delivers the most difficult un-annotated sentence pairs or the easiest ones. The user can also choose not to use this difficulty score for selecting sentences to annotate, but to use the original corpus order of the sentences. There is also a forth option in the drop-down lists, which lets the user search for a specific word in the corpus, and annotate all sentence pairs in which this word is included.

---

sequence of characters to be considered a subword, but this figure should also be allowed to be adjusted to the language pairs used.

[5]https://github.com/robertostling/efmaral

[6]https://www.nltk.org/_modules/nltk/translate/gdfa.html

4. Concluding remarks

With line-a-line, we have provided a tool that we hope will form a useful resource for annotating word-alignments in sentence-aligned parallel corpora.[7]

Whether the pre-annotations available will have a quality that is high enough to be found helpful when annotating, will depend on the resources available, i.e. on which language pairs that are to be aligned, on the size of the parallel corpus available, and on the quality of the multilingual word embedding space. A key functionality of the line-a-line tool is therefore to provide several methods for pre-annotation, and let the user choose the one that is found most helpful for performing the annotation.

For instance, we perceived the pre-annotations constructed by a union of intersection-symmetrising and dictionary creation alignments to be most useful during the tool development. In contrast, pre-annotations constructed through the GDFA symmetrisation were perceived as not useful, as they contained too many false positives for our small Swedish-German parallel corpus.

Acknowledgements

This work was funded by the Swedish Research Council (project number 2017-00626).

5. Bibliographical References

Alkhouli, T., Bretschner, G., Peter, J.-T., Hethnawi, M., Guta, A., and Ney, H. (2016). Alignment-based neural machine translation. In *ACL 2016 First Conference on Machine Translation*, pages 54–65, Berlin, Germany, August.

Axelrod, A., Mayne, R. B., Callison-burch, C., Osborne, M., and Talbot, D. (2005). Edinburgh system description for the 2005 IWSLT speech translation evaluation. In *In Proc. International Workshop on Spoken Language Translation (IWSLT)*.

Bird, S. (2002). NLTK: The natural language toolkit. In *Proceedings of the ACL Workshop on Effective Tools and Methodologies for Teaching Natural Language Processing and Computational Linguistics*, Stroudsburg, PA, USA. Association for Computational Linguistics.

Bourgonje, P., Hoek, J., Evers-Vermeul, J., Redeker, G., Sanders, T., and Stede, M. (2018). Constructing a lexicon of Dutch discourse connectives. *Computational Linguistics in the Netherlands Journal*, 8:163–175, 12/2018.

Conneau, A., Lample, G., Ranzato, M., Denoyer, L., and Jégou, H. (2017). Word translation without parallel data. *arXiv preprint arXiv:1710.04087*.

Dahl, Ö. and Wälchli, B. (2016). Perfects and iamitives : two gram types in one grammatical space. *Letras de Hoje*, 51(3):325–348.

Dahlberg, S. and Domeij, R. (2017). Översättning av termer i myndighetstexter: En studie om översättning av myndighetstermer i arbetet med nationell språkinfrastruktur på språkrådet. In *Workshop Termplanering och termbruk i svenskan på Svenskans beskrivning 36*.

---

[7]The tool will be made freely available at: https://github.com/mariask2/line-a-line.

Dahlberg, S. (2017). Tre svenska myndigheters strategier för termöversättning till spanska och franska. Bachelor's thesis, Stockholm University, Department of Linguistics.

Hung-Ngo, Q. and Winiwarter, W. (2012). A visualizing annotation tool for semi-automatically building a bilingual corpus. In *The Fifth Workshop on Building and Using Comparable Corpora (5th BUCC within the LREC2012)*, pages 67–74.

Merkel, M., Petterstedt, M., and Ahrenberg, L. (2003). Interactive word alignment for corpus linguistics. In *Proceedings of Corpus Linguistics 2003, 28-31st March, 2003, Lancaster UK. UCREL Technical Papers.*, pages 533–542. UCREL (University Centre for Computer Corpus Research on Language). ISBN 1 86220 131 5.

Östling, R. and Tiedemann, J. (2016). Efficient word alignment with Markov Chain Monte Carlo. *The Prague Bulletin of Mathematical Linguistics*, 106:125–146, 10.

Pourdamghani, N., Ghazvininejad, M., and Knight, K. (2018). Using word vectors to improve word alignments for low resource machine translation. In *Proceedings of the 2018 Conference of the North American Chapter of the Association for Computational Linguistics: Human Language Technologies, Volume 2 (Short Papers)*, pages 524–528, New Orleans, Louisiana, June. Association for Computational Linguistics.

Skeppstedt, M., Kucher, K., Stede, M., and Kerren, A. (2018). Topics2Themes: Computer-Assisted Argument Extraction by Visual Analysis of Important Topics. In *Proceedings of the LREC Workshop on Visualization as Added Value in the Development, Use and Evaluation of Language Resources*, pages 9–16.

Stasko, J. (2008). Jigsaw: Investigative analysis on text document collections through visualization. In *DESI II: Second International Workshop on Supporting Search and Sensemaking for Electronically Stored Information in Discovery Proceedings*.

Tiedemann, J., Cap, F., Kanerva, J., Ginter, F., Stymne, S., Östling, R., and Weller-Di Marco, M. (2016). Phrasebased SMT for Finnish with more data, better models and alternative alignment and translation tools. In *Proceedings of the First Conference on Machine Translation: Volume 2, Shared Task Papers*, pages 391–398, Berlin, Germany, August. Association for Computational Linguistics.

Wirén, M., Matsson, A., Rosén, D., and Volodina, E. (2018). Svala: Annotation of second-language learner text based on mostly automatic alignment of parallel corpora. In *Selected papers from the CLARIN Annual Conference 2018, Pisa, 8-10 October 2018*, number 159, pages 227–239. Linköping University Electronic Press, Linköpings universitet.

Zhang, Y., Wang, Z., Uchimoto, K., Ma, Q., and Isahara, H. (2008). Word alignment annotation in a Japanese-Chinese parallel corpus. In *LREC 2008*.

Proceedings of the 13th Workshop on Building and Using Comparable Corpora, pages 6–13
Language Resources and Evaluation Conference (LREC 2020), Marseille, 11–16 May 2020
© European Language Resources Association (ELRA), licensed under CC-BY-NC

Overview of the Fourth BUCC Shared Task:
Bilingual Dictionary Induction from Comparable Corpora

Reinhard Rapp
Athena R.C. and Magdeburg-Stendal
University of Applied Sciences
and University of Mainz
reinhardrapp@gmx.de

Pierre Zweigenbaum
Université Paris-Saclay
LIMSI, CNRS
91400 Orsay, France
pz@limsi.fr

Serge Sharoff
University of Leeds
Leeds, LS2 9JT
United Kingdom
s.sharoff@leeds.ac.uk

Abstract

The shared task of the 13th Workshop on Building and Using Comparable Corpora was devoted to the induction of bilingual dictionaries from comparable rather than parallel corpora. In this task, for a number of language pairs involving Chinese, English, French, German, Russian and Spanish, the participants were asked to determine automatically the target language translations of several thousand source language test words in three frequency ranges. We describe here some background, the task definition, the training and test data sets and the evaluation used for ranking the participating systems. We also summarize the approaches used and present the results of the evaluation. In conclusion, the outcome of the competition is the results of a number of systems which provide surprisingly good solutions to an ambitious problem.

Keywords: bilingual dictionary, lexicon induction, comparable corpora

1. Introduction

In the framework of machine translation, the extraction of bilingual dictionaries from parallel corpora has been conducted very successfully (see e.g. Mihalcea & Pedersen, 2003). But on the other hand, human second language acquisition appears not to be based on parallel data. This means that there must be a way of acquiring and relating lexical knowledge across two or more languages without the use of parallel data.

It has been suggested that it may be possible to extract multilingual lexical knowledge from comparable rather than from parallel corpora (see e.g. Sharoff et al., 2013). From a theoretical perspective, this suggestion may lead to advances in understanding human second language acquisition. From a practical perspective, as comparable corpora are available in much larger quantities than parallel corpora, this approach might help in relieving the data acquisition bottleneck which tends to be especially severe when dealing with language pairs involving low resource languages (see e.g. Martin et al., 2005).

A well-established practical task to approach this topic is bilingual lexicon extraction from comparable corpora, which is in the focus of this shared task. Typically, its aim is to extract word translations such as exemplified in Table 1 from comparable corpora, where a given source word may receive multiple translations. Note that, to reflect the tabular format used in the shared task, multiple translations of the same source word are listed in separate rows.

Quite a few research groups have been working on this problem using a wide variety of approaches. There are comprehensive studies such as Irvine & Callison-Burch (2017) and also overview papers at least in part discussing the topic like Jakubina & Langlais (2016), Rapp et al. (2016), Sharoff et al. (2013).

Source (English)	Target (French)
baby	bébé
baby	poupon
bath	bain
bed	lit
bed	plumard
convenience	commodité
doctor	médecin
doctor	docteur
eagle	aigle
mountain	montagne
nervous	nerveux
work	travail

Table 1: Sample word translations from English to French. In the shared task a similar tab-separated format was used.

However, as up to now there was no standard way to measure the performance of the systems, the published results are not comparable and the pros and cons of the various approaches are not clear.

2. Shared Task Description

The present shared task[1] aimed at solving these problems by organizing a fair competition between systems. This was accomplished by providing corpora and bilingual datasets for a number of language pairs involving Chinese, English, French, German, Russian and Spanish, and by comparing the results using a common evaluation framework. For the shared task we provided corpora as well as training and test data. However, as we anticipated that these corpora and datasets may not suit all needs, we divided the shared task into two tracks:

- In the *closed track*, participants were required to only use the data provided by the organizers. In this way equal conditions were ensured and, as the outcome of

---

[1] https://comparable.limsi.fr/bucc2020/bucc2020-task.html

this track, the systems could be compared and ranked according to the quality of their results.

- In the *open track*, participants were free to use their own corpora and training data. If possible, they were supposed to still use the evaluation data provided in the closed track, but this was also not mandatory. The participants could even work on languages for which the shared task provided no data. If relevant, the participants were supposed to describe why their systems were not suitable for the closed track, and discuss the pros and cons of their choices. They were also encouraged to provide access to their data for the purpose of facilitating replication by others.

To give an overview on the steps to be conducted by the participating teams, Table 2 provides a checklist for the participants in an abbreviated form. The time schedule is shown in Table 3. With about three weeks, the time span between the release of the test sets and the submission of the final results was (in comparison to most other shared tasks) foreseen to be relatively long for the reason that some teams worked on more language pairs than others and would have been at a disadvantage if this time span had been a limiting factor (but it probably still was to some extent).

- Decide on the track and the language pairs.
- Express your interest to the shared task organizers. You may also suggest new language pairs, and we might be able to help you with data.
- Download the corpora from the shared task webpage (WaCky or Wikipedia)
- Download the training data (bilingual word pairs) for your language pairs from the shared task webpage.
- Run your system on the words on the source side of the training data and compute the translations. Compare your results with target side of the training data and improve your system if necessary.
- Download the test data on the date specified in the time schedule.
- Run your system on the test data. Format your output in the same way as you see in the training data.
- Before the deadline specified in the schedule, submit your results.
- Write and submit a system description paper.
- Present your paper at the workshop.

Table 2: Checklist for participants (abbreviated).

Any time	Expressions of interest to participate in the shared task
January 12, 2020	Release of shared task training sets
February 16, 2020	Release of shared task test sets
March 5, 2020	Submission of shared task results

Table 3: Time schedule.

---

3. Closed Track

3.1 Corpora

Table 4 lists the corpora to be used for the language pairs supported in the closed track. Due to their free availability for several languages and their size, for the shared task we used the WaCky-corpora kindly provided by the Web-as-a-corpus initiative[2] (Baroni et al., 2009) and cleaned-up versions of Wikipedia dumps.

The cells in Table 4 show which of the two types of corpora were supposed to be used for the two languages of a language pair when conducting the dictionary induction task. The rationale behind these choices is that the WaCky corpora, with a greater variety of topics and genres, seem somewhat better suited for the dictionary induction task than Wikipedia, but they are not available for Chinese and Spanish. Language pairs involving Chinese and Spanish therefore use Wikipedia, whereas other language pairs use WaCky.

	de	en	es	fr	ru	zh
de		deWaC ukWaC	deWiki esWiki	deWaC frWaC		
en	ukWaC deWaC		enWiki esWiki	ukWaC frWaC	ukWaC ruWaC	enWiki zhWiki
es	esWiki deWiki	esWiki enWiki				
fr	frWaC deWaC	frWaC ukWaC				
ru		ruWaC ukWaC				
zh		zhWiki enWiki				

Table 4: Language pairs supported and corpora (WaCky or Wikipedia) to be used in the closed track.

The WaCky corpora are cleaned-up web crawls. Their compressed sizes are: English: 3.2 GB, French: 3.0 GB, German; 3.0 GB, Russian: 4.1 GB. English, French, and German are supposed to comprise in the order of 2 billion, Russian about 3 billion running words (Sharoff et al., 2017).

The compressed sizes of the Wikipedia corpora are: English: 3.6 GB, Spanish: 0.9 GB, Chinese: 0.4 GB. They are in a one-line per document format. The first tab-separated field in each line contains metadata, the second field contains the text. Paragraph boundaries are marked with HTML tags. As cleaning up the original Wikipedia dump files is not trivial, occasionally there can be some noise in the form of not fully cleaned HTML and Javascript fragments. Details of the cleanup and preparation procedure can be found in Sharoff et al. (2015).

3.2 Embeddings

For the convenience of the shared task participants, we provided pre-trained fastText embeddings for all WaCky and Wikipedia corpora listed in Table 4. They were trained

---

[2] http://wacky.sslmit.unibo.it/doku.php?id=corpora

on the Wikipedia or WaCky corpora and were allowed to be readily used in both tracks.

The fastText embeddings for the Wikipedia corpora were taken from Facebook AI Research (Bojanowsky et al., 2017).[3] For the WaCky-corpora, pre-trained fastText embeddings were computed and made available by Serge Sharoff as follows:

- The .vec.xz files are text representations, widely used in various tools.
- The .bin files are binary versions for use in fastText.
- The following parameters were used: method: skipgram; minCount: 30; dim: 300; ws (context window): 7; epochs: 10; neg (number of negatives sampled): 10. The other parameters are the defaults for fastText.

3.3 Training and test datasets

For training and testing the systems, reasonable numbers of bilingual word pairs as exemplified in Table 1 had to be provided for the language pairs listed in Table 4. Alexis Conneau from Facebook AI Research kindly gave us permission to use for the shared task extracts from the MUSE "Ground-truth bilingual dictionaries"[4] as described in Conneau et al. (2017). In this paper, the authors describe their data as follows:

> "**Word translation** The task considers the problem of retrieving the translation of given source words. The problem with most available bilingual dictionaries is that they are generated using online tools like Google Translate, and do not take into account the polysemy of words. Failing to capture word polysemy in the vocabulary leads to a wrong evaluation of the quality of the word embedding space. Other dictionaries are generated using phrase tables of machine translation systems, but they are very noisy or trained on relatively small parallel corpora. For this task, we create high-quality dictionaries of up to 100k pairs of words using an internal translation tool to alleviate this issue. We make these dictionaries publicly available as part of the MUSE library"

To us, the MUSE data on word translations looks like being derived from word-aligned parallel corpora by filtering out infrequent and therefore less reliable translations of a source language word. In particular, as it seems that for each source language word at most five possible translations are provided, it appears that only those target language translations which are aligned to at least 20% of the occurrences of a given source language word are listed.[5]

For more than 100 language pairs, the MUSE data lists such word translations. The lists use UTF-8 encoding and lower case characters only. Apparently, they are sorted by descending corpus frequencies of the source language words. As an example, Table 5 shows the top 40 lines of the list for English–German. For some language pairs, blanks are used as separators between source word and translation, but tabs for others. Although this is not applicable to the current shared task, to provide for future extensions to multiword units, we unified this to tabs.

English	German	English	German
the	die	utc	utc
the	der	his	seinem
the	dem	his	seinen
the	den	his	seine
the	das	his	sein
and	sowie	his	seiner
and	und	not	not
was	war	not	nicht
was	wurde	not	kein
for	für	are	sind
that	dass	talk	vortrag
that	das	talk	gespräch
with	mit	talk	reden
from	vom	talk	talk
from	von	which	welches
from	ab	which	welcher
from	aus	which	welche
this	dieser	which	welchen
this	diese	also	ausserdem
this	das	also	ebenso

Table 5: Top 40 translations from the English to German MUSE word translation data.

Table 6 gives, in alphabetical order according to ISO-language codes,[6] an overview of the number of bilingual word pairs (lines in the files) provided for each of the language pairs in the MUSE word translation data.[7] As can be seen in column *Lines*, this number varies between 20549 (ko-en) and 113324 (fr-en). However, as many source language words have several translations, the number of unique source language words (word types) is smaller. Column *Types* shows that this number varies between 13727 (ko-en) and 106473 (es-pt). Comparing the two columns gives an idea of the average number of translations for each source language word of a language pair.

Rather than providing one large set of training data for each language pair, by splitting into three frequency ranges we provide three equally-sized smaller sets per language pairs. Looking at different frequency ranges is of scientific interest as algorithms typically work best for high or medium frequency words, whereas the performance at low frequencies is often of higher practical relevance.

---

[3] https://fasttext.cc/docs/en/pretrained-vectors.html

[4] https://github.com/facebookresearch/MUSE

[5] We are extrapolating from what we did ourselves in the previous COMTRANS project, which, however, covered only a few language pairs (https://cordis.europa.eu/project/id/23845)

[6] https://en.wikipedia.org/wiki/List_of_ISO_639-1_codes

[7] As of May 2020, the MUSE website lists dictionaries for 110 language pairs (see https://github.com/facebookresearch/MUSE). However, there is a double occurrence of the en-en file (identical files with the same English words on the source and the target side). We list this file only once in our table which is why we have only 109 items in Table 6.

Lang.	Lines	Types	Lang.	Lines	Types
af-en	37421	36054	en-tr	67799	58901
ar-en	31355	24547	en-uk	47912	39365
bg-en	55170	45769	en-vi	77020	74447
bn-en	23829	19165	en-zh	39334	32495
bs-en	43318	40997	es-de	68869	59839
ca-en	78081	76720	es-en	112583	96579
cs-en	64211	55867	es-fr	87297	86765
da-en	81959	70776	es-it	96290	95406
de-en	101997	78200	es-pt	107363	106473
de-es	68905	64574	et-en	32776	28527
de-fr	61527	60802	fa-en	41321	33914
de-it	59811	59373	fi-en	43102	35770
de-pt	54765	54554	fr-de	61517	61119
el-en	45515	37186	fr-en	113324	97021
en-af	37446	35000	fr-es	87310	87010
en-ar	33663	22305	fr-it	97719	97121
en-bg	61240	49447	fr-pt	94552	92193
en-bn	30737	25564	he-en	45679	36735
en-bs	43333	38784	hi-en	31046	25732
en-ca	78097	74867	hr-en	56424	51305
en-cs	64216	52554	hu-en	42823	34974
en-da	82018	67177	id-en	96518	83355
en-de	101931	74655	it-de	59798	59686
en-el	56070	45152	it-en	103613	93214
en-en	92844	92844	it-es	96284	91929
en-es	112580	93084	it-fr	97711	92706
en-et	32748	27514	it-pt	91869	91503
en-fa	48164	41327	ja-en	25969	21003
en-fi	43055	32061	ko-en	20549	13727
en-fr	113286	94681	lt-en	33435	31807
en-he	47333	38070	lv-en	46385	40419
en-hi	38221	31719	mk-en	43935	36620
en-hr	56413	47834	ms-en	73092	66469
en-hu	42868	34944	nl-en	93853	84583
en-id	96500	86656	no-en	75171	70035
en-it	103612	90589	pl-en	73901	64397
en-ja	35353	31580	pt-de	54737	54534
en-ko	22357	17517	pt-en	108686	97261
en-lt	33447	30595	pt-es	107351	102289
en-lv	46407	37250	pt-fr	94517	88109
en-mk	50749	40580	pt-it	91849	91370
en-ms	73087	68548	ro-en	80821	75407
en-nl	93835	82181	ru-en	48714	40486
en-no	75204	66098	sk-en	65878	56408
en-pl	73883	59952	sl-en	62890	54894
en-pt	108696	92504	sq-en	52090	45534
en-ro	80815	68749	sv-en	82348	71678
en-ru	53186	42615	ta-en	21230	18247
en-sk	65887	50917	th-en	25332	21567
en-sl	62907	51473	tl-en	34984	32284
en-sq	52111	40853	tr-en	68611	58040
en-sv	82372	68608	uk-en	40723	34888
en-ta	26656	22610	vi-en	76364	73445
en-th	24658	22386	zh-en	21597	13768
en-tl	34980	31463			

Table 6: Number of bilingual word pairs (lines) and number of unique source language words (types) for each language pair in the MUSE word translation data. The ratio between lines and types can be seen as a measure of the average fertility (number of translations) of the source language words.

We split the data into three parts corresponding to frequency ranges of the source language words: The high frequency range provides bilingual word pairs where the frequency is among the 5000 most frequent words in the MUSE data. The mid frequency range consists of words ranking between 5001 and 20000, and the low frequency range belongs to ranks 20001 to 50000. However, for languages where the MUSE data comprises less than 50000 unique source language words (see Table 6), we had to reduce these thresholds. For en-ru and ru-en the thresholds were set to 5000, 20000 and 40000. For en-zh they are at 5000, 15000 and 30000, and for zh-en they are at 4500, 9000 and 13500.

From these ranges we extracted (pseudo) random samples which we call bins. Each bin comprises 2000 unique source language words together with all their translations. Like in the original MUSE data, also in the bins the source language words are ordered according to frequency (most frequent first). All three sets (per language pair) taken together, this gives 6000 unique source language words together with their translations, whereby, as shown in Table 5, each possible translation is listed in a separate line along with the source language word.

Given large datasets and an ambitious shared task schedule, we did not have the time to manually correct the data files. However, although the MUSE dictionaries were apparently generated automatically, they seem mostly of reasonably good quality, with only few errors. An exception is the low frequency range of English-Chinese where almost all source language words are translated by identical target language words which is not very useful. We encouraged the participants of the shared task to report to us such errors so that, as a positive side effect of the shared task, information for the improvement of the datasets was collected. For details, see the system description papers of the shared task participants in this volume.

For testing the systems, lists of source language test words were provided which, based on word frequency, were likewise split into three sets of 2000 unique words.

We had informed the participants that if their algorithms required a seed lexicon, they should use an arbitrary part of the training data for this purpose. Our hope was that with its 6000 source language words and even more translation pairs, the training set was large enough to provide for the participants' needs. If not, participants were referred to the open track of the shared task.

4. Open Track

In this track, participants were free to work on other language pairs, use their own data and, if desired, use their own evaluation procedures. They were encouraged to describe in their papers the reasons and motivation for deviating from the procedures of the closed track and, if possible, to provide access to their data. We also indicated that we might be able to give support for other language pairs by providing cleaned-up Wikipedia corpora and datasets of word translations extracted from MUSE.

Note that the limited choice of language pairs in the closed track was deliberate in order not to scatter participation over too many languages with the consequence of making comparisons between systems difficult. But in principle we were prepared to offer support for all language pairs covered by the MUSE dictionaries.

As this appears to be the first shared task on the topic of dictionary induction from comparable corpora, we could not draw on previous experiences. Due to this pilot character, in Track 1 we were trying to keep things as clear and unsophisticated as possible. But in Track 2 we encouraged participants to challenge this simplicity, to freely experiment and to come up with new ideas in the hope that the resulting insights will promote future progress in the field.

5. Participants and Systems

Despite the ambitious schedule of the shared task, four teams managed to submit their results in time. These teams and the tracks and language pairs they worked on are listed in Table 7. As cited in the table, the first three teams have system description papers in this volume, which is why we only briefly describe their approaches here.

Short name	Long name / paper	Track and language pairs
CEN	Amrita School of Engineering, Center for Computational Engineering and Networking (CEN) (Sanjanasri et al., 2020)	*closed track:* de-en *open track:* ta-en
LMU	LMU Munich, Center for Information and Language Processing (Severini et al., 2020)	*closed track:* de-en, en-de, en-ru, ru-en *open track:* de-en, en-de, en-ru, ru-en
LS2N	Université de Nantes, TALN/LS2N (Laville et al., 2020)	*closed track:* de-en, en-de, de-fr, fr-de, en-es, es-en, en-fr, fr-en
SW	Sida Wang[8]	*closed track:* en-zh, zh-en

Table 7: Participating teams and their tracks and language pairs.

The LMU team relies on bilingual word embeddings which they claim to be effective in low resource settings. However, as they typically do not perform well on low frequency words, the embeddings are supplemented utilizing word surface similarity such as orthography and transliteration information.

The LS2N team combines a word embedding approach with a concatenation approach based on Tomas Mikolov's well known Word2vec[9] system together with a cognates matching approach based on string similarity.

The CEN team puts an emphasis on the transfer learning of semantics based on cross-lingual embeddings. For this purpose they experiment with different approaches, such as Word2Vec, Multilayer Perceptrons and Convolutional Neural Networks.

Sida Wang described his system as follows:[10]

"1) The system does not use the training data for training, instead it uses identical mappings as initialization and uses the training set as a validation set

2) An iterative procedure is used to figure out as much of the vocabulary as possible, independent of what is needed in the output (i.e. independent of the test set)
2a) I used the supervised rotation method where nearest neighbors (corrected with CSLS) are predicted as translations
2b) The iterative procedure adds (s,t) if t $\in$ top_k(s) and t $\in$ top k(t) where a k of 2 did the best on the validation set

3) My implementation is based on vecmap (https://github.com/artetxem/vecmap) but I only used a supervised procedure and a different iterative procedure as described above"

6. Evaluation

For evaluation, participants of the closed track (for the open track this was optional) were asked to provide their results on the test data sets for the test words in each of the three frequency ranges. Hereby it was expected that for each source language word all its major translations were provided (whereby the definition of "major" was supposed to be inferred from the training data). These translations were compared to the translations as found in the (internal) gold standard data which is structurally similar to the training data as it was randomly sampled from the same MUSE data in the same three frequency ranges. Only identical strings were considered correct, and the performance of a system was determined by computing precision (P), recall (R), and F1-score, the latter being the official score for system ranking. All data sets are in UTF-8 encoding.

More precisely: the input to the system is a list of source language words, one per line. A system was supposed to return, for each input word one or more candidate translations, in the form of tab-separated word pairs, each on its own line. For instance, in the English-French case, given the gold standard, test word list, and system output as shown in Table 8, the system would get credited for two true positives, one false positive, and two false negatives, hence

$$P = 2 / 3 = 0.67$$

$$R = 2 / 4 = 0.50$$

$$F1 = 2 (P * R) / (P + R) = 0.57$$

---

[8] http://www.sidaw.xyz/, https://www.linkedin.com/in/sidaw
[9] https://en.wikipedia.org/wiki/Word2vec

[10] E-mail to shared task organizers (May 2, 2020).

Table 9 shows some pseudo-code for computing these scores in a very simple and efficient way. The implementation can be conducted using standard UNIX commands such as *sort* and *wc*.

gold standard	
bed	lit
bed	plumard
doctor	médecin
doctor	docteur

test set
bed
doctor

system output	
bed	lit
bed	futon
doctor	docteur

Table 8: Sample gold standard, test word list and system output for the English-French case.

```
Inputs:
    File with system output
    File with gold standard data

Assumptions:
    Tab-separated word pairs in both files (as in Table 1)
    Only unique lines in both files (no repetitions)

Procedure:
    A = number of lines in file with system output
    B = number of lines in file with gold standard data
    C = A + B
    Merge both input files
    Conduct unique sort of the lines in the merged file
    D = number of lines in uniquely sorted file
    NoMatches = C − D
    R = NoMatches / B
    P = NoMatches / A
    F1 = 2 * (P * R) / (P + R)
```

Table 9: Pseudo code for computing recall, precision and F1-score.

7. Results

7.1 Overall results (without considering frequency bins)

Table 10 show the participating teams' results for the closed track. These are overall results not considering the frequency bins, i.e. when the data from the three frequency bins are merged for the gold standard data and also for the system output data. Table 11 shows analogous data for the open track. No evaluation was conducted for CEN's ta-en (Tamil-English) language pair as we had not provided a test set for this.

Overall results closed track				
Lang.	Team	R	P	F1
de-en	CEN	15.3	5.2	7.7
	LMU	48.7	61.6	54.4
	LS2N	57.5	66.2	61.5
en-de	LMU	40.2	59.8	48.1
	LS2N	54.3	54.8	54.5
en-ru	LMU	33.9	37.8	35.8
	LS2N[11]	32.6	38.7	35.4
		37.8	*30.7*	*33.9*
ru-en	LMU	43.9	56.7	49.5
	LS2N	35.5	56.7	43.7
de-fr	LS2N	76.8	76.7	76.8
fr-de	LS2N	78.3	64.9	71.0
en-es	LS2N	63.8	61.4	62.6
es-en	LS2N	67.5	75.1	71.1
en-fr	LS2N	61.2	69.7	65.1
fr-en	LS2N	46.0	64.6	53.7
en-zh	SW	45.3	54.6	49.5
zh-en	SW	33.6	40.9	36.9

Table 10: Overall results for the closed track.

Overall results open track				
Lang.	Team	R	P	F1
de-en	LMU	50.6	63.8	56.4
en-de	LMU	41.1	61.1	49.2
en-ru	LMU	39.3	43.8	41.4
ru-en	LMU	50.7	65.4	57.1

Table 11: Overall results for the open track.

7.2 Results when considering frequency bins

Tables 12 to 15 show the teams' results when the high/mid/low frequency bins are distinguished. Again, no evaluation was conducted for CEN's ta-en (Tamil-English) language pair. Given the difficulty of the task where the teams not only had to rank candidates but also had to precisely decide which ones to keep and which ones to discard, we found the best results surprisingly good.

Concerning the frequencies of the source language words, often the results get better with lower frequencies, showing that the methods are quite good in dealing with sparse data. Only the low frequency words of the language pair zh-en, with an astonishing F1-score of 0.852, benefits from an idiosyncrasy of the MUSE data: Here almost all items consist of identical strings on the source and target language sides, which is particularly beneficial for the approach used by Sida Wang (see section 5).

---

[11] Normal font: Results based on overall file (no distinction of frequency bins) as provided by team. Italics: Results from merged high/mid/low-frequency bins. Bins provided by team.

| Closed track by frequency | | | | | | | | | |
| Lang. | Team | high freq. | | | mid freq. | | | low freq. | | |
		R	P	F1	R	P	F1	R	P	F1
de-en	CEN	9.0	4.0	5.5	15.0	4.9	7.4	27.0	6.6	10.6
de-en	LMU	44.7	49.1	46.8	43.4	70.9	53.8	62.8	77.1	69.2
de-en	LS2N	48.1	63.7	54.8	59.0	63.0	60.9	72.2	73.3	72.8
en-de	LMU	35.1	51.4	41.7	35.0	65.3	45.6	61.4	71.2	66.0
en-de	LS2N	49.0	51.6	50.3	53.7	52.6	53.2	68.6	65.2	66.9
en-ru	LMU	38.0	41.0	39.4	30.7	39.1	34.4	29.5	30.3	29.9
en-ru	LS2N	47.7	36.5	41.3	34.3	25.7	29.4	21.4	22.5	22.0
ru-en	LMU	45.3	67.6	54.2	45.5	59.4	51.5	39.9	43.1	41.4
ru-en	LS2N	49.3	59.0	53.7	38.3	56.0	45.5	13.2	48.8	20.8

Table 12: Comparison of results by frequency for the closed track.

| Closed track by frequency LS2N | | | | | | | | | |
| Lang. | high freq. | | | mid freq. | | | low freq. | | |
	R	P	F1	R	P	F1	R	P	F1
de-fr	73.0	66.8	69.8	78.8	76.9	77.8	78.9	89.5	83.8
fr-de	73.9	50.2	59.8	79.1	67.0	72.6	82.0	85.9	83.9
en-es	57.6	61.7	59.6	63.3	56.8	59.9	77.8	67.1	72.1
es-en	61.9	74.9	67.8	66.4	72.8	69.4	77.2	78.0	77.6
en-fr	55.2	66.2	60.2	59.9	67.6	63.5	74.4	78.5	76.4
fr-en	54.6	65.6	59.6	49.1	64.3	55.7	29.4	62.0	39.8

Table 13: Results by frequency for the closed track for language pairs where only LS2N participated.

| Closed track by frequency SW | | | | | | | | | |
| Lang. | high freq. | | | mid freq. | | | low freq. | | |
	R	P	F1	R	P	F1	R	P	F1
en-zh	39.1	40.9	40.0	27.0	41.5	32.7	78.1	93.8	85.2
zh-en	40.1	50.1	44.5	32.9	47.3	38.8	25.6	25.6	25.6

Table 14: Results by frequency for the closed track for language pairs where only SW participated.

| Open track by frequency LMU | | | | | | | | | |
| Lang. | high freq. | | | mid freq. | | | low freq. | | |
	R	P	F1	R	P	F1	R	P	F1
de-en	44.6	49.0	46.6	46.7	76.2	57.9	66.4	80.8	72.9
en-de	35.4	51.8	42.0	36.8	68.6	47.9	62.5	72.3	67.1
en-ru	36.8	39.7	38.2	36.1	46.0	40.4	48.5	49.9	49.2
ru-en	46.9	70.0	56.2	50.3	65.5	56.9	56.3	60.7	58.4

Table 15: Results by frequency for the open track for language pairs where only LMU participated.

8.   Conclusions and Outlook

The fourth BUCC shared task addressed the extraction of bilingual dictionaries from comparable corpora. This is a difficult task as, in contrast to parallel corpora, in this case it is not clear how to bridge the gap between languages. Nevertheless, the best participating systems achieved consistently good results for a number of language pairs involving languages from related as well as from very distant languages.

Of course, the provided datasets were not perfect: They were based on the automatically created MUSE dictionaries and, due to their considerable sizes, not manually checked. For each of 28 language pairs they comprised 12000 unique source language words (6000 for the training sets and another 6000 for the test sets) with somewhat more translations.

Challenges of interest for future shared tasks on bilingual lexicon induction from comparable corpora include:

1)   Finding mappings across the full set of inflected forms of two languages. For example, *adequate* in English maps to four cognate forms in Spanish: *adecuado, adecuada, adecuados, adecuadas*, corresponding to the choices of singular vs. plural and feminine vs. masculine, because the English adjectives do not inflect for number and gender. The gold standard we used in the current shared task did not necessarily include the full range of forms.

2)   Another issue concerns the representation of word senses in the test set. Since the gold standard translations were extracted from parallel corpora, as word selection in the target language is biased by the words in the source language, their set is likely to be different from what is available in general comparable corpora, such as the WaCky corpora and Wikipedia. For example, translations of *strong voice* extracted from the Europarl corpus primarily include references to expressions of opinions rather than assessments of the vocal cord. Translations also exhibit a cline from clear homonymy for words like *bank* to clear polysemy for words like *heavy* in which the same sense can be translated slightly differently depending on the context *heavy luggage, heavy blow, heavy rain*. More research is needed into what is the range of polysemous translations in the available test datasets.

3)   In preparing data for this shared task we used information about the frequencies of words, as highly frequent words exhibit different translation properties from low frequent words. However, the test lexicon contains other sources of variation, which are worth a separate investigation, such as common names, borrowings or proper names. For example, borrowed proper names have sometimes trivial translations, e.g. *Kazimierz* maps to itself in the English to French evaluation set.

4)   A particularly relevant topic is multiword expressions which are omnipresent in specialized language. We did not address them at all here, but this should certainly be a fruitful direction of research in the future.

9.   Acknowledgements

We would like to thank Alexis Conneau from Facebook AI Research for allowing us to use extracts of the MUSE word translation data for the shared task and the Web-as-a-corpus initiative for providing the WaCky-corpora.

This work was partially funded by the Marie Curie Career Integration Grant MULTILEX within the 7th European Community Framework Programme and by the Marie Curie Individual Fellowship SEBAMAT within the European Commission's Horizon 2020 Framework Programme.

9. Bibliographical References

Baroni, Marco; Bernardini, Silvia; Ferraresi, Adriano; Zanchetta, Eros (2009). The WaCky wide web: A collection of very large linguistically processed web-crawled corpora. *Language Resources and Evaluation* 43 (3): 209–22.

Bojanowski, Piotr; Grave, Edouard; Joulin, Armand; Mikolov, Tomas (2017). Enriching word vectors with subword information. *Transactions of the Association for Computational Linguistics*, Vol. 5, 135 –146.

Conneau, Alexis; Lample, Guillaume; Ranzato, Marc'Aurelio; Denoyer, Ludovic; Jégou, Hervé (2017). Word translation without parallel data. *arXiv preprint arXiv: 1710.04087* (published at ICLR 2018).

Irvine, Ann; Callison-Burch, Chris (2017). A comprehensive analysis of bilingual lexicon induction. *Computational Linguistics* 43 (2), 273–310.

Jakubina, Laurent; Langlais, Philippe (2016). A comparison of methods for identifying the translation of words in a comparable corpus: recipes and limits. *Computación y Sistemes* 20 (3), 449–458.

Laville, Martin; Hazem, Amir; Morin, Emmanuel (2020). TALN/LS2N participation at the BUCC shared task: bilingual dictionary induction from comparable corpora. *Proceedings of the 13th Workshop on Building and Using Comparable Corpora.*

Martin, Joel; Mihalcea, Rada; Pedersen, Ted (2005). Word alignment for languages with scarce resources. *Proceedings of the ACL Workshop on Building and Using Parallel Texts.*

Mihalcea, Rada; Pedersen, Ted (2003). An evaluation exercise for word alignment. *Proceedings of the HLT-NAACL 2003 Workshop on Building and Using Parallel Texts: Data Driven Machine Translation and Beyond.*

Rapp, Reinhard; Sharoff, Serge; Zweigenbaum, Pierre (2016). Recent advances in machine translation using comparable corpora. *Journal of Natural Language Engineering* 22 (4), 501–516.

Sanjanasri, JP; Menon, Vijay Krishna; Soman, KP (2020). BUCC 2020: bilingual dictionary induction using cross-lingual embedding. *Proceedings of the 13th Workshop on Building and Using Comparable Corpora.*

Severini, Silvia; Hangya, Viktor; Fraser, Alexander; Schütze, Hinrich (2020). LMU bilingual dictionary induction system with word surface similarity scores for BUCC 2020. *Proceedings of the 13th Workshop on Building and Using Comparable Corpora.*

Sharoff, Serge; Goldhahn, Dirk; Quasthoff, Uwe (2017). *Frequency Dictionary: Russian.* Leipziger Universitätsverlag. http://corpus.leeds.ac.uk/serge/publications/2017-russian-frq-leipzig.pdf

Sharoff, Serge; Rapp, Reinhard; Zweigenbaum, Pierre (2013). Overviewing important aspects of the last twenty years of research in comparable corpora. In: Serge Sharoff, Reinhard Rapp, Pierre Zweigenbaum, Pascale Fung (eds.): Building and Using Comparable Corpora. Heidelberg: Springer, 1–18.

Sharoff, Serge; Rapp, Reinhard; Zweigenbaum, Pierre (2013). Overviewing important aspects of the last twenty years of research in comparable corpora. In: Serge Sharoff, Reinhard Rapp, Pierre Zweigenbaum, Pascale Fung (eds.): *Building and Using Comparable Corpora.* Heidelberg: Springer, 1–18.

Sharoff, Serge; Zweigenbaum, Pierre; Rapp, Reinhard (2015). BUCC shared task: cross-language document similarity. *Proceedings of the Eighth Workshop on Building and Using Comparable Corpora*, Beijing, China. ACL Anthology, 74–78, http://www.aclweb.org/anthology/W15-3411.pdf

Proceedings of the 13th Workshop on Building and Using Comparable Corpora, pages 14–21
Language Resources and Evaluation Conference (LREC 2020), Marseille, 11–16 May 2020
© European Language Resources Association (ELRA), licensed under CC-BY-NC

Constructing a Bilingual Corpus of Parallel Tweets

Hamdy Mubarak, Sabit Hassan, Ahmed Abdelali
Qatar Computing Research Institute
Doha, Qatar
{hmubarak, sahassan2, aabdelali}@hbku.edu.qa

Abstract

In a bid to reach a larger and more diverse audience, Twitter users often post *parallel tweets* —tweets that contain the same content but are written in different languages. Parallel tweets can be an important resource for developing machine translation (MT) systems among other natural language processing (NLP) tasks. In this paper, we introduce a generic method to collect parallel tweets. Using this method, we collect a bilingual corpus of Arabic-English parallel tweets and a list of Twitter accounts who post Arabic-English tweets regularly. Since our method is generic, it can also be used for collecting parallel tweets that cover less-resourced languages such as Urdu or Serbian. Additionally, we annotate a subset of Twitter accounts with their countries of origin and topic of interest, which provides insights about the population who post parallel tweets. This latter information can also be useful for author profiling tasks.

Keywords: Corpus Creation, Machine Translation, Arabic-English, Parallel Tweets, Comparable Corpora

1. Introduction

Extensive usage of social media in recent years has flooded the web with a massive amount of user-generated content. This has the potential to be a very valuable resource for Natural Language Processing (NLP) tasks such as Machine Translation (MT). However, in social media platforms such as Twitter, users typically write content in a very informal way. The users extensively use emoticons, short forms of phrases such as "idk (I don't know)" and follow traits that are far from traits of traditionally written content that follow language rules and grammar closely. Because of the unpredictable and inconsistent nature of content in social media, it is quite difficult to exploit this type of data. In recent years, this issue has gained significant interest among researchers and motivated many of them to work on harvesting useful data from this ever-growing pool of user-generated content. To facilitate this process, we identify and focus on an interesting trait among Twitter users: some Twitter users post tweets with the same message written in different languages —that we will call *parallel tweets*.

Organizations, celebrities and public figures on social media platforms, such as Twitter, try to reach out to as large of an audience as possible. Often the audience consists of individuals who use different languages. To build a connection with this diverse audience, organizations, celebrities, and public figures post tweets in multiple languages to ensure max reach out. Twitter, with traditionally 140 (Now, 280) character limit on the tweets, prompts the users to reach out to their audiences across multiple tweets containing the same message in different languages. In our paper, we propose a method to collect such tweets. These parallel tweets can be a great resource for machine translation. Ling et al., (2013) show that parallel texts from Twitter can significantly improve MT systems. As opposed to crowdsourcing translations that cost money or complex mechanisms of cross-language information retrieval, we provide a free and generic method of obtaining a large amount of translations that cover highly sought after new vocabulary and terminology. For example, in Table 1, we can see that, خدمة إلكترونية is translated to "e-Service" by the user.

Google Translate on the other hand, would translate it as "electronic service".

In our proposed method, we first crawl Twitter to collect a large number of tweets and find unique Twitter accounts from these tweets. Then, we filter the accounts to only include those who are likely to post parallel tweets —accounts with high popularity. Then, for each account, we identify candidates for parallel tweets and lastly, we filter the candidate parallel tweets to only include tweets that have a high possibility of being parallel. For filtering candidate parallel tweets, we use a simple dictionary based method along with some heuristics. We also eliminate parallel tweets with repetitive content as we want our collection to capture the diversity of user-generated content on social media without redundancy in the collection.

In this paper, we focus on collecting pairs of Arabic-English parallel tweets using the proposed method. We release 166K pairs of Arabic-English parallel tweets. We also report 1389 accounts that post such parallel tweets regularly. This collection of accounts is valuable as we expect these accounts to continue posting parallel tweets in the future. To demonstrate this effect, we collect parallel tweets from the same users in two different time frames, separated by 16 months, and observe a remarkable growth in the number of parallel tweets collected. This suggests that our resource will grow significantly in the future. We publicly share the parallel tweets by their IDs as well as the usernames of Twitter accounts who post parallel tweets regularly.

A phenomenon similar to parallel tweets is *comparable tweets*. When a pair of tweets have significant overlap in content and theme but are not exact translations of each other, we call them *comparable tweets*. Since our method is automatic, it is prone to some errors. In our error analysis (section 4), we notice that although some pairs of tweets that were tagged as parallel by our system may not be exact translations of each other, they are actually comparable tweets. Since these pairs of tweets have significant overlap, they can also be useful for many tasks in cross-language information retrieval.

In addition to collecting parallel tweets and Twitter accounts, we also annotate a subset of Twitter accounts for their countries and topics the accounts typically post about. This allows us to understand the demographics of Twitter users who post parallel tweets. This information will be useful in future collections of parallel tweets as we will know in which countries posting parallel tweets is a popular trend and which topics are likely to have many parallel tweets. Moreover, this information can be useful for tasks such as author profiling.

Although in our paper, we present a bilingual corpus of Arabic-English parallel tweets, our generic method can also be adapted for other language pairs and has the potential to be particularly useful for less-resourced languages such as Urdu or Serbian.

In section 2, we survey related work from relevant literature, and in section 3, we present our method and data collected using this method. In section 4, we provide some preliminary assessments for the data quality, and in section 5, we discuss the annotation of accounts for their countries of origin and topics of tweets. Lastly, we conclude with a summary and future work.

2.   Related Work

Although the amount of data on social media is growing at an incredible speed and can be a valuable resource for NLP tasks, the utilization of data on social media has been underwhelming. Efforts to use these platforms as a resource for translation are still relatively small.

Sluyter Gäthje et al. (2018) built a parallel resource for English-German using 4000 English tweets that were manually translated into German with a special focus on the informal nature of the tweets. The objective was to provide a resource tailored for translating user generated-content.

Jehl et al. (2012) and Abidi and Smaili (2017) extract parallel phrases by using CLIR techniques. The major difference is that these methods are extracting comparable data, whereas, we want to extract parallel tweets, which we can expect to be closer to true translation. Jehl et al. use a probabilistic translation-based retrieval (Xu et al., 2001) in the context of Twitter for the purpose of training Statistical Machine Translation (SMT) pipeline. For evaluation purposes, Jehl et al. (2012) use crowdsourcing to create a parallel corpus of 1000 Arabic tweets and 3 manual English translations for each Arabic tweet and reports improvement for SMT pipeline. Abidi and Smaili (2017) used topics related to Syria to crawl Twitter and collect 58,000 Arabic tweets and 60,000 English tweets. The tweets are then preprocessed heavily, which requires knowledge of Arabic. Then, the tweets are aligned to produce a corpus of comparable Arabic-English tweets aimed at improving MT systems.

Vicente et al. (2016) present a parallel corpus that covers 5 languages from the Iberian Peninsula, created by automatic collection and crowdsourcing. To align parallel content, Vicente et al. (2016) use measures such as publication date, string length similarity, hashtag and user mention overlap, and Longest Common Subsequence ratio (LCSR). LCSR exploits the similarity of the languages within the Iberian peninsula. The aim of the corpus is to aid in the development of microtext translation systems. Vicente et al. (2016) used the corpus in a shared task to evaluate it.

In comparison to the above methods, our method is more generic, which does not require specific knowledge of the language and can be used for different language pairs. Our method is also relatively simple that uses minimal external resources. The generic and simple nature of our method makes it easily adaptable for less-resourced languages.

Ling et al. (2013) collect parallel content of different languages from single tweets (compare Table 1 and Table 2 for difference). They reported a significant improvement in MT systems. In this work, we will not focus on extracting parallel content from single tweets. However, our methods can be adapted to do so in the future.

Our work also augments existing work in Twitter account annotation. Specifically for Arabic Twitter users, there is a scarcity of resources. Inspired by Mubarak and Darwish (2014), who annotate tweets for their dialects, Bouamor et al. (2019) presented a dataset of 3000 Twitter accounts annotated with their countries of origin. Alhozaimi and Almishari (2018) categorize 80 Twitter accounts into 4 categories of topics the accounts are interested in. It suffices to say that there is a need for such resources and our annotation of Twitter accounts for country and topic, although not our primary goal, is a step forward.

3.   Methodology and Corpus Construction

Before diving further into the methodology, it's important to have a good understanding of the phenomenon of parallel tweets. In this section, we will provide details of the phenomenon on Twitter and the various options used by the platform users, followed by our methodology and details of collected corpus.

3.1.   Parallel Tweets

If a pair of tweets are translations of each other, we call them parallel tweets. It's important to distinguish between parallel tweets and tweets that contain parallel data. Table 1 and Table 2 contain examples of parallel tweets and tweets containing parallel content respectively. Our focus is on the scenario of Table 1. We can identify several characteristics of parallel tweets that are important for developing the methodology. We observe that the tweets are usually consecutive or within a short period of time. The presence of certain words in both tweets can indicate that they are parallel tweets. It suffices to check if there is a significant overlap between the two tweets.

3.2.   Methodology

Our methodology follows a three-step procedure. First, we collect candidate parallel tweets from Twitter users who are likely to post parallel tweets. In the second step, we filter candidate parallel tweets to obtain our collection of parallel tweets. In order to improve the quality of the corpus, in the third step, we remove duplicate tweets and exclude accounts who post repetitive tweets.

3.2.1.   Collecting Candidate Parallel Tweets

Step 1: search Twitter for a large number of tweets using commonly appearing words in the targeted language pair, alternatively, we can use language filter if available; e.g

Account	Country	Language	Tweet
HukoomiQatar	Qatar	English	e-Service | The Ministry of Economy and Commerce provides a number of services to the Qatari nationals
		Arabic	خدمة إلكترونية | تقدم وزارة الاقتصاد والتجارة مجموعة من الخدمات للمواطنين القطريين
ArifAlvi	Pakistan	English	I pray for the quick recovery of Mr Nawaz Sharif. May Allah restore him to full health. I am sure the government will ensure all medical facilities.
		Urdu	میں نواز شریف صاحب کی جلد صحت یابی کلئی اللہ کی بارگاہ میں دعا گو ہوں اور امید کرتا ہوں کہ حکومت تمام طبی سہولات کی فراہمی یقنی بنائی گی
SerbianPM	Serbia	English	Sam Parker, Congratulations to @vonderleyen and the new Commission team. We look forward to working with you over the next five years as we prepare Serbia for EU Membership.
		Serbian	Честитке @vonderleyen и новом тиму Европске комисије. Радујемо се што ћемо сарађивати са вама у наредних пет година док припремамо Србију за чланство у ЕУ.

Table 1: Examples of parallel tweets

Account	Country	Language	Tweet
SerbianPM	Serbia	Serbian	Поносна сам на представљање најбољих српских производа у економском Павиљону на другом кинеском међународном сајму увоза ЕКСПО у Шангају #СИЕ #Србија
		English	Proud to see the best of #Serbia on display at the Economic Pavilion of the China International Import Expo in Shanghai #CIIE
KuwaitAirways	Kuwait	Arabic	احجز مع العطلات إلى المدينه المنورة على عروض درجه رجال الأعمال،، للمزيد من المعلومات اتصل على 1806060
		English	Book your trip to Madinah with our Business Class offers For more information call 1806060

Table 2: Examples of tweets with parallel content (inside same tweet)

"lang:ar" in case of Arabic. **Step 2:** Collect all the unique accounts from these tweets. **Step 3:** At this point, it's important to understand who is likely to post parallel tweets. Our assumption is that most likely the Twitter user will have a large number of followers. In this step, we shortlist the accounts based on number of followers. **Step 4:** We collect all available tweets from the shortlisted accounts but exclude tweets that are too short as they would compromise the richness of the corpus. **Step 5:** For each tweet, we check language of the tweet along with language of previous and next tweet as we expect the user to post parallel tweets within a short period of time. If the languages form our target pair of languages, we consider the corresponding tweets to be candidate parallel tweets.

3.2.2. Filtering Candidate Parallel Tweets

Once we have the candidate tweets, we need to identify which ones are indeed parallel tweets. In our language pair, let us call the first language L1, and second language L2. We assume availability of a dictionary that maps words from L1 to L2. In our candidate pair of parallel tweets, let us call the tweet from L1 to be T1 and the tweet from L2 to be T2.

Step 1: We remove stopwords from both tweets[1]. **Step 2:** We remove commonly known suffixes and prefixes from words of T1 and T2 and assume the remaining parts are stems.[2] Such surface-level (and light) stemming yields reasonably good result while being easily applicable to less-resourced languages. We anticipate that using complex stemmer/lemmatizer or a high-coverage lookup table when available would yield better accuracy of the collected tweets, but we opted to examine the accuracy of our approach in low-resourced scenario where these resources are typically unavailable. **Step 3:** We look up stems of T1 in the dictionary and check if the stem appears in T2 after mapping from L1 to L2. If it does, we count it as a "match". **Step 4:** If the number of matches exceeds a threshold, we tag the pair as parallel tweets.

The matching threshold in step 4 can be changed to obtain corpus of different quality. Higher threshold will result in higher quality corpus, but lower number of parallel tweets. To decide this threshold, we take a subset of the data and annotate it manually, identifying if they are indeed parallel. Then, we plot number of parallel tweets retained for

---

[1] https://sites.google.com/site/kevinbouge/stopwords-lists

[2] Example: in our English surface stemming, we just removed 's', 'ed' and 'ing' from the end of words.

Correctness	English tweet	Arabic tweet
Correct	GOAL! Scored by Chang Jin Moon (Shabab Al Ahli Dubai) 35 min. Shabab Al Ahli Dubai 1 Emirates 0 #SAHvEMR	هدف! سجله شانج جن مون (شباب الأهلي دبي) دقيقة 35.شباب الأهلي دبي 1 الإمارات 0 #SAHvEMR
Wrong	GOAL! Scored by Chang Jin Moon (Shabab Al Ahli Dubai) 35 min. Shabab Al Ahli Dubai 1 Emirates 0 #SAHvEMR	نهاية الشوط الأول: شباب الأهلي دبي 1 الإمارات 0 #SAHvEMR (Translation: The end of the first half: Shabab Al Ahli Dubai 1 Emirates 0 #SAHvEMR)

Table 3: Example of duplicate tweets

Account	English tweet	Arabic tweet
QatarPrayer	It's now **Fajer** athan time **4:05am** according to Doha city local time and its suburbs. #Qatar	حان الآن موعد أذان الفجر 4:05 ص حسب التوقيت المحلي لمدينة الدوحة وضواحيها. #قطر
	It's now **Asr** athan time **3:06pm** according to Doha city local time and its suburbs. #Qatar	حان الآن موعد أذان العصر 3:06م حسب التوقيت المحلي لمدينة الدوحة وضواحيها. #قطر

Table 4: Example of account posting repetitive tweets. Differences between English tweets (templates) are written in bold.

different thresholds and the corresponding errors.

3.2.3. Improving Quality of Corpus

At this point, we noticed that, since each tweet is compared with its preceding and succeeding tweet, it's possible that the tweet has matching words exceeding the threshold for both the previous and next tweet. Table 3 illustrates this issue[3]. This is an uncommon occurrence but to address this issue, we pick the pair that has a higher number of matches. We also noticed that some accounts posted repetitive tweets that are extremely similar to each other. These accounts mostly follow a template for posting tweets and are likely to be bots. Table 4 shows an example of such accounts. These accounts are not very useful for the purpose of creating a corpus for machine translation. To identify these accounts, we plot number of words in all the tweets posted by the account against the number of unique words among them. If the ratio of unique words versus total words is below a threshold, we exclude the account.

To increase the quality of the collected Arabic-English tweets, we can use complex Arabic word segmenter to split prefixes and suffixes, for example Farasa word segmenter (Darwish and Mubarak, 2016; Abdelali et al., 2016), or lemmatizer (Mubarak, 2018), and for English we can use Porter stemmer (Porter, 1980). We leave this for future work.

3.3. Arabic-English Parallel Tweets Corpus

Using the method described in Section 3.2., we collect a corpus of 166K Arabic-English parallel tweets and 1,389 accounts who regularly post them. For our collection of Arabic-English parallel tweets, first, we collect 175M Arabic tweets in March 2014 using Twitter API with language filter assigned to Arabic; "lang:ar". From these tweets, we identify 15,000 unique accounts who have more than 5,000 followers and collect available tweets from these accounts. Since very short tweets (less than or equal to 5 words) are not that useful for many NLP tasks such as MT, we exclude them from our collection. Once we have a large number of tweets, we carry out the procedure in Section 3.2. in two stages, separated by 16 months. During the first stage, we collect 120K parallel tweets from these accounts in July 2018. We expect these accounts to continue to post parallel tweets. Therefore, in November 2019, we collect parallel tweets from the same accounts again. During this stage, we collect more than 83K additional pairs of tweets. At this point, we have 203K parallel tweets. We can see that our collection grew significantly in the span of 16 months. Therefore, we can expect the collection to grow further in the future. To illustrate possible growth in the future, Table 5 shows the top 5 accounts (according to the number of parallel tweets collected) and their posting rate of parallel tweets. To reduce the margin of error, we removed duplicates from the collection as described in Section 3.2. During the whole procedure, we use Buckwalter Lexicon (Buckwalter, 2004) as a dictionary to calculate degree of matching between two tweets. If the degree of matching exceeds threshold of *3*, we consider the tweets to be parallel. The matching threshold of 3 is found experimentally and justified in section 4.

Then, we calculate ratio of unique words and total number of words in tweets posted by each account. If this ratio falls below the threshold of 0.1, we exclude the account and all the tweets posted by the account. This threshold is also decided on experimentally, which is described in section 4. Finally, we end up with 166K tweets posted by 1,389 accounts.

---

[3]In all tables, in case of wrong English translation, the correct translation is given inside parentheses.

4. Quality of Corpus

In order to determine the quality of our collected corpus and identify the thresholds described in section 3, we select a subset of candidate parallel tweets and annotate them manually. To select this subset of tweets, we notice that, after removal of short tweets, the average number of words in tweets is 23. We randomly select 1,000 pairs of tweets who match on at least 10% of the mean number of words (rounded up, 10% of 23 is 3). We categorize these 1,000 tweets as "parallel" (translations of each other), "comparable" (they have significant overlap in content) or "unrelated" (errors) manually. Table 6 shows examples of the different categories.

Figure 1 depicts experimentation on degree of matching used as threshold to decide whether a pair is indeed parallel. In Figure 1, we group tweets that are parallel and comparable together and consider unrelated tweets as errors. We can see that at threshold of 3, we achieve less than 10% error rate. Going from threshold of 3 to 4, we lose 22.3% (from 1,000 to 777) of the tweets while reducing the error by only 2% (from 95 out of 1,000, which is 9.5%, to 58 out of 777, which is 7.5%). We can see the trend that when the threshold is increased, we lose a significant portion of tweets, while reducing error by only a small fraction. Since with threshold of 3, we retain large number of tweets while having less than 10% error rate, we decide that 3 is an appropriate threshold for our corpus.

Account	Number of Parallel tweets	Rate of Posting (Per Day)
HukoomiQatar	2,615	3.18
culturebah	2,311	1.69
AshghalQatar	2,202	2.16
DMunicipality	1,974	2.23
QF	1,944	2.11

Table 5: Accounts with highest posting rate of parallel tweets

To identify accounts who post repetitive tweets, we calculate the ratio of unique words and total words posted by accounts. If the ratio falls below a threshold, we consider the account to post repetitive content. In order to find an appropriate threshold, we plot the ratio of number of unique words and total words for each account against number of tweets posted by that account. We can see from Figure 2 that there are few accounts who have a high number of tweets and fall below the ratio of 0.1. KuwaitMet is one such account (posted ∼7,000 tweets, with ratio less than 0.01). KuwaitMet is the official account of Kuwait Meteorological Department. They post many tweets every day using a template-like format that differ only in certain values such as wind speed or rain amount, while rest of tweet content is the same. Parallel tweets from such accounts are not desirable as they do not contribute to the richness of corpus and therefore, we exclude them from our corpus.

To understand the coverage of our corpus, we count the total number of words (Tokens) and number of unique words (Types) in the set of English and Arabic tweets separately.

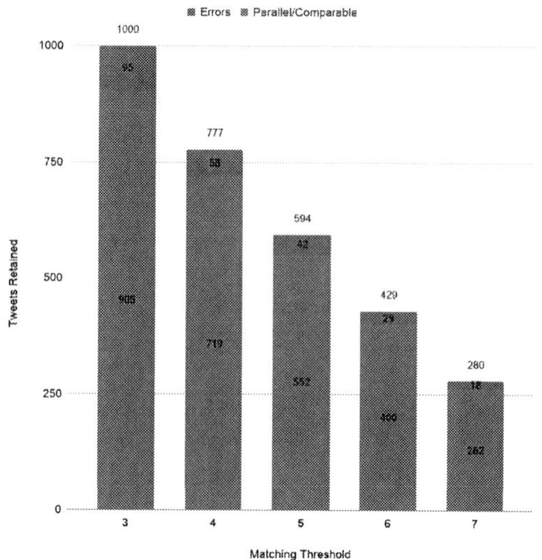

Figure 1: Error comparison of matching threshold

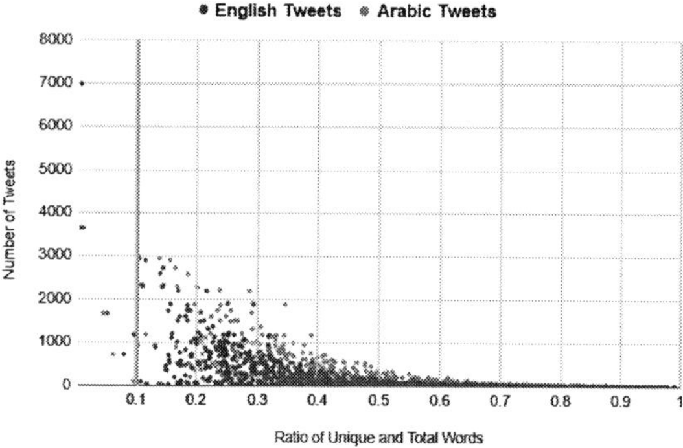

Figure 2: Number of tweets vs. ratio of unique words. Threshold (in Green) for discarded accounts and their respective volume of words.

Table 8 shows this information. The large number of unique words is expected as Twitter users write in different styles and use many words that are not found in the dictionary.

The trade-off in our method for improving accuracy and ratio of unique and total words is the number of tweets. If the thresholds is too high in the above cases, we will lose a significant amount of data.

Table 7 shows evaluation of the final corpus that we present on the 1,000 manually annotated pairs of tweets. We can see that with our current settings, we obtain reasonably good performance as, 68.1% are indeed parallel tweets, 22.4% tweets that are comparable and only 9.5% pairs are errors. If we group parallel and comparable tweets together, we achieved 90.5% accuracy.

Lastly, to address the concern regarding the translation quality as well as the originality of these translations, we evaluate how the parallel tweets compare with Google Translate using MT evaluation metrics such as BLEU score, NIST, Translation Edit Rate (TER) and Word Error Rate (WER). We take a random 100 pairs of parallel tweets.

Category	English tweet	Arabic tweet
Parallel	#LGgram - one of the lightest laptops in the world! Can you guess its weight?	جهاز #LGgram هو أنحف كمبيوتر محمول في العالم ! هل تستطيع أن تحزر وزنه؟
Comparable	@k_seghir advices freshmen to follow their passion whilst enjoying the educational journey. Learn both inside and outside the classroom.	مدير الجامعة يدعو الطلبة الجدد للاستمتاع في رحلتهم التعليمية داخل وخارج القاعات الدراسية. (Translation: The university president invites new students to enjoy their educational journey inside and outside the classroom)
Error	Live: The press conference begins with a tour through Dilmun Hall.	مباشر: معالي الشيخة مي تؤكد بأن اختيار قاعة دلمون لعقد المؤتمر الصحفي لما له من دلالة على اثار البحرين. (Translation: Live: Her Excellency Sheikha Mai confirms that the choice of Dilmun Hall to hold the press conference...)

Table 6: Examples of corpus evaluation

Parallel Tweets	Comparable Tweets	Unrelated Tweets
68.1%	22.4%	9.5%

Table 7: Evaluation of the corpus

Accts	Tweets	English		Arabic	
		Tokens	Types	Tokens	Types
1,389	166K	3.8M	380K	3.6M	450K

Table 8: Corpus statistics

BLEU	NIST	TER	WER
27.74	4.55	72.47	77.23

Table 9: Comparison of parallel tweets with Google Translate output

The English tweets from these 100 pairs are used as reference. The Arabic tweets from these 100 pairs are used as input to Google Translate and the outputs from Google Translate are compared with the reference tweets using the above metrics. This comparison is summarized in Table 9. The moderately low values of BLEU score and NIST, along with moderately high TER and WER also suggest that these parallel tweets are indeed human translations.

IDs of parallel tweets, list of Twitter accounts and manual annotation can be downloaded from the Qatar Computing Research Institute resources page `http://alt.qcri.org/resources` or the direct link: `http://bit.ly/2xApE8V`

5. Country and Topic Annotation

To understand the demographics of users who post parallel tweets, we annotate the top 200 accounts, who contribute to 80% of total collected parallel tweets, for their countries of origin and topics of interest. This annotation can be useful for other purposes such as author profiling as well.

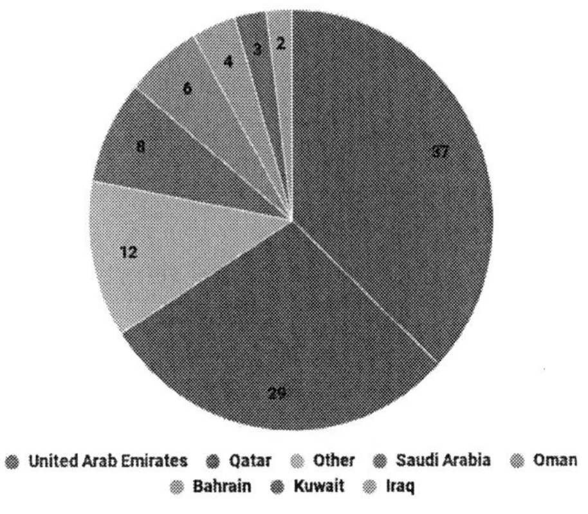

Figure 3: Distribution of accounts according to country

5.1. Country Annotation

We annotate the accounts for their countries of origin. This is not always straightforward as Twitter users may use different kinds of location names on their profiles. We consider city name, country name or flags to get an indication of the country for the account. The distribution of countries is presented in Figure 3. We can see that posting parallel tweets is particularly popular in the Gulf region (UAE, Qatar for example). In the Gulf region, both English and Arabic are used extensively as the population is multilingual. Therefore, we can expect other multilingual communities to be a potential source for parallel tweets as well.

5.2. Topic Annotation

We also annotate the accounts for a topic they are most likely to tweet on. This is done by going through the Twitter profile and identifying the most common topic across tweets. We assign one topic to a profile and categorize

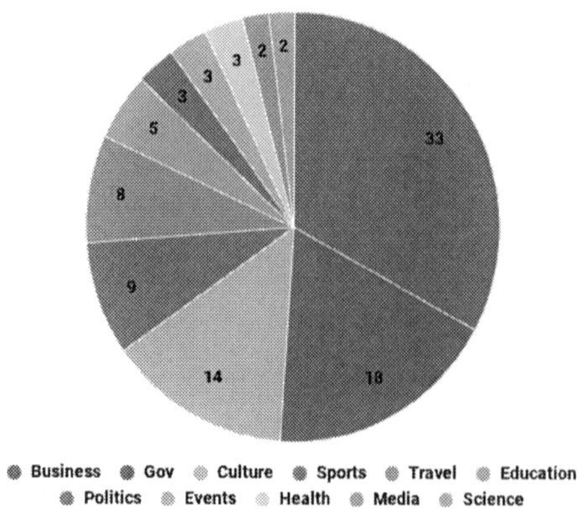

Figure 4: Distribution of accounts according to topic

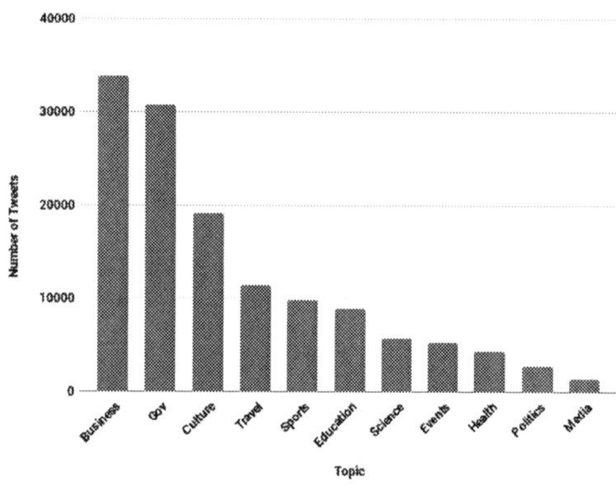

Figure 5: Distribution of tweets according to topic

tweets by that profile to be of that topic. Although the accounts may post tweets related to different topics, for our purposes, a broad understanding of the distribution at the tweet level suffices. Figure 4 shows us the distribution of topics across profiles and Figure 5 shows us the tweet distribution. We can see that majority of the parallel tweets are posted by business (corporations, banks, companies, etc.) or government entities (embassies, ministries, municipalities, etc.) This information can help us in the future to refine our search for accounts who post parallel tweets. During the annotation process, we noticed an interesting phenomenon. Some government or business entities do not post parallel tweets from the same account but use different accounts to post tweets that are translations of each other. For example, the accounts MoI_Qatar and MoI_Qatar_En are two accounts maintained by the same government entity (Ministry of Interior). While MoI_Qatar posts tweets in Arabic, MoI_Qatar_En posts same content translated into English. This has the potential to be an additional resource for parallel tweets and our method can be adapted in future to get those accounts and obtain more parallel tweets.

6.   Conclusion and Future Work

In this paper, we have presented a method for collecting parallel tweets of different languages. Using this method, we have collected a bilingual corpus of Arabic-English tweets with over 166K parallel tweets. Although our method has a margin of error, we evaluated how different thresholds can be adjusted to increase accuracy or improve quality of corpus. In addition to the listing of accounts who post such tweets, we have also annotated these accounts with their respective countries of origin and topic that they are likely to tweet on. In the future, we plan to assess the impact of adding such resource to MT systems and use complex stemmer/lemmatizer to improve corpus quality and study its effect on MT performance. We also plan to replicate the same efforts and method to collect data for less-resourced languages.

7.   Bibliographical References

Abdelali, A., Darwish, K., Durrani, N., and Mubarak, H. (2016). Farasa: A fast and furious segmenter for arabic. In *Proceedings of NAACL-HLT 2016 (Demonstrations)*, pages 11–16. Association for Computational Linguistics.

Abidi, K. and Smaili, K. (2017). How to match bilingual tweets ? In *6th NLP 2017 - Computer Science Conference Proceedings in Computer Science & Information Technology (CS & IT)* , Computer Science Conference Proceedings in Computer Science & Information Technology (CS & IT), Sydney, Australia, February.

Alhozaimi, A. and Almishari, M. (2018). Arabic twitter profiling for arabic-speaking users. *2018 21st Saudi Computer Society National Computer Conference (NCC)*, pages 1–6.

Bouamor, H., Hassan, S., and Habash, N. (2019). The MADAR shared task on Arabic fine-grained dialect identification. In *Proceedings of the Fourth Arabic Natural Language Processing Workshop*, pages 199–207, Florence, Italy, August. Association for Computational Linguistics.

Buckwalter, T. (2004). *Buckwalter Arabic Morphological Analyzer Version 2.0 LDC2004L02.Web Download.* Philadelphia: Linguistic Data Consortium.

Darwish, K. and Mubarak, H. (2016). Farasa: A new fast and accurate arabic word segmenter. In *Proceedings of the Tenth International Conference on Language Resources and Evaluation (LREC'16)*, pages 1070–1074.

Jehl, L., Hieber, F., and Riezler, S. (2012). Twitter translation using translation-based cross-lingual retrieval. In *Proceedings of the Seventh Workshop on Statistical Machine Translation*, pages 410–421, Montréal, Canada, June. Association for Computational Linguistics.

Ling, W., Xiang, G., Dyer, C., Black, A., and Trancoso, I. (2013). Microblogs as parallel corpora. In *Proceedings of the 51st Annual Meeting of the Association for Computational Linguistics (Volume 1: Long Papers)*, pages 176–186, Sofia, Bulgaria, August. Association for Computational Linguistics.

Mubarak, H. and Darwish, K. (2014). Using twitter to collect a multi-dialectal corpus of Arabic. In *Proceedings of the EMNLP 2014 Workshop on Arabic Natural Lan-*

guage Processing (ANLP), pages 1–7, Doha, Qatar, October. Association for Computational Linguistics.

Mubarak, H. (2018). Build fast and accurate lemmatization for arabic. In *Proceedings of the Eleventh International Conference on Language Resources and Evaluation (LREC 2018)*.

Porter, M. F. (1980). An algorithm for suffix stripping. *Program*, 14(3):130–137.

Sluyter-Gäthje, H., Lohar, P., Afli, H., and Way, A. (2018). FooTweets: A bilingual parallel corpus of world cup tweets. In *Proceedings of the Eleventh International Conference on Language Resources and Evaluation (LREC 2018)*, Miyazaki, Japan, May. European Language Resources Association (ELRA).

Vicente, I. S., Alegría, I., España-Bonet, C., Gamallo, P., Oliveira, H. G., Garcia, E. M., Toral, A., Zubiaga, A., and Aranberri, N. (2016). TweetMT: A parallel microblog corpus. In *Proceedings of the Tenth International Conference on Language Resources and Evaluation (LREC'16)*, pages 2936–2941, Portorož, Slovenia, May. European Language Resources Association (ELRA).

Xu, J., Weischedel, R., Weischedel, R., and Nguyen, C. (2001). Evaluating a probabilistic model for cross-lingual information retrieval. In *Proceedings of the 24th Annual International ACM SIGIR Conference on Research and Development in Information Retrieval*, SIGIR '01, pages 105–110, New York, NY, USA. ACM.

Proceedings of the 13th Workshop on Building and Using Comparable Corpora, pages 22–28
Language Resources and Evaluation Conference (LREC 2020), Marseille, 11–16 May 2020
© European Language Resources Association (ELRA), licensed under CC-BY-NC

Automatic Creation of Correspondence Table of Meaning Tags from Two Dictionaries in One Language Using Bilingual Word Embedding

Teruo Hirabayashi[*], **Kanako Komiya**[*], **Masayuki Asahara**[†], **Hiroyuki Shinnou**[*]

[*]Ibaraki University
4-12-1 Nakanarusawa, Hitachi, Ibaraki JAPAN
{18nm736g, kanako.komiya.nlp, hiroyuki.shinnou.0828}@vc.ibaraki.ac.jp

[†]National Institute for Japanese Language and Linguistics
10-2 Midoricho, Tachikawa, Tokyo, JAPAN
masayu-a@ninjal.ac.jp

Abstract

In this paper, we show how to use bilingual word embeddings (BWE) to automatically create a corresponding table of meaning tags from two dictionaries in one language and examine the effectiveness of the method. To do this, we had a problem: the meaning tags do not always correspond one-to-one because the granularities of the word senses and the concepts are different from each other. Therefore, we regarded the concept tag that corresponds to a word sense the most as the correct concept tag corresponding the word sense. We used two BWE methods, a linear transformation matrix and VecMap. We evaluated the most frequent sense (MFS) method and the corpus concatenation method for comparison. The accuracies of the proposed methods were higher than the accuracy of the random baseline but lower than those of the MFS and corpus concatenation methods. However, because our method utilized the embedding vectors of the word senses, the relations of the sense tags corresponding to concept tags could be examined by mapping the sense embeddings to the vector space of the concept tags. Also, our methods could be performed when we have only concept or word sense embeddings whereas the MFS method requires a parallel corpus and the corpus concatenation method needs two tagged corpora.

Keywords: Bilingual Word Embedding, Concept Embeddings, Word Embeddings, Dictionary

1. Introduction

Recently, corpora that have tags from more than one tag set are increasing. For example, "The Balanced Corpus of Contemporary Written Japanese" (BCCWJ) (Maekawa et al., 2014) is tagged with concept tags from "Word List by Semantic Principles" (WLSP) (National Institute for Japanese Language and Linguistics, 1964) after tagged with sense tags from "Iwanami Kokugo Jiten (Nishio et al., 1994)."

Because these tags are tagged referring to different dictionaries, the word senses of a word are different from each other. However, both tagging schemes are common in a way, that is, a unique meaning is given to every word in the corpus. Wu (Wu et al., 2019) created a corresponding table of word senses from Iwanami Kokugo Jiten and concept numbers form WLSP manually. If we could this process automatically, tagging of corpora would be much easier. Therefore, in this paper, we describe how to utilize bilingual word embeddings (BWE) to automatically create a corresponding table of meaning tags from two dictionaries in one language, Japanese, and examine the effectiveness of the method.

2. Related Work

BWE is classified into four groups according to how to make cross-lingual word embeddings [1]. First approach is monolingual mapping. These approaches initially train monolingual word embeddings and learn a transformation matrix that maps representations in one language to those of the other language. Mikolov et al. (Mikolov et al.,

2013b) have shown that vector spaces can encode meaningful relations between words and that the geometric relations that hold between words are similar across languages. Because they do not assume the use of specific language, their method can be used to extend and refine dictionaries for any language pairs. Second approach is pseudo-cross-lingual. These approaches create a pseudo-cross-lingual corpus by mixing contexts of different languages. Xiao and Guo (Xiao and Guo, 2014) proposed the first pseudo-cross-lingual method that utilized translation pairs. They first translated all words that appeared in the source language corpus into the target language using Wiktionary. Then they filtered out the noises of these pairs and trained the model with this corpus in which these pairs are replaced with placeholders to ensure that translations of the same word have the same vector representation. Third approach is cross-lingual training. These approaches train their embeddings on a parallel corpus and optimize a cross-lingual constraint between embeddings of different languages that encourages embeddings of similar words to be close to each other in a shared vector space. Hermann and Blunsom (Hermann and Blunsom, 2014) trained two models to output sentence embeddings for input sentences in two different languages. They retrained these models with sentence embeddings using a least-squares method. Final approach is joint optimization. They not only consider a cross-lingual constraint, but also jointly optimize mono-lingual and cross-lingual objectives. Klementiev et al. (Klementiev et al., 2012) was the first research using joint optimization. Zou (Zou et al., 2013) used a matrix factorization approach to learn cross-lingual word representations for English and Chinese and utilized the representa-

---

[1] http://ruder.io/cross-lingual-embeddings/

tions for machine translation task. In this paper, we train BWE model by monolingual mapping and create a correspondence table of meaning tags using the model. To our knowledge, this research is the first research that uses BWE to find correspondences of meaning tags in one language.

3. Methods

Usually, BWE is used for cross-lingual applications, e.g., machine translation. The word embeddings trained from a parallel corpus, a comparable corpus, or two monolingual corpora are necessary for BWE. On the other hand, the number of corpora that were tagged by more than one tag sets is increasing. One corpus could have tags of part of speeches, word senses, named entities, and so on. We can regard a corpus that was tagged with two tag sets as a parallel corpus. For example, a corpus that was tagged with the meaning tags of two dictionaries in one language would be regarded as a parallel corpus of the meaning tag sets of two dictionaries.

In this research, we show how to utilize BWE to automatically find the correspondences of meaning tags in one language and investigate the effectiveness of the method. We generated two sets of word embeddings from a corpus with two meaning tags from different dictionaries. After that, we find correspondences of the meanings from two dictionaries using BWE. We used BCCWJ with concept tags from WLSP and sense tags from Iwanami Kokugo Jiten for the experiments. Both the word sense of Iwanami Kokugo Jiten and the concept number of WLSP represent a meaning of words and both of them are classified using a tree structure. The meaning tags do not always correspond one-to-one because the granularities of the word senses and the concepts are different from each other. However, the final purpose of this research is to automatically create a correspondence table between the word senses and the concept tags. We regarded the concept tag that corresponds to a word sense the most as the correct concept tag corresponding the word sense.

3.1. Sense Tags from Iwanami Kokugo Jiten

Iwanami Kokugo Jiten is a Japanese monolingual dictionary. In Iwanami Kokugo Jiten, each word sense has a sense tag such as "17877-0-0-1-0", composed of "headline ID"-"compound word ID"-"large classification ID"-"medium classification ID"-"small classification ID." When word sense has no corresponding ID, it would be 0. For example, the word senses and their corresponding sense tags of a word "子供 (child or children)" are listed in Table 1 [2].

Table 1: Word Senses and Their Corresponding Sense Tags of "子供 (Child or Children)" from Iwanami Kokugo Jiten[4]

Sense Tag	Word Sense
17877-0-0-1-0	<1> 幼い子。児童。 Young person. Someone who is not yet an adult. Kid.
17877-0-0-2-0	<2> 自分のもうけた子。むすこ、むすめ。子。 Son/daughter. A son or daughter of any age.

Figure 1 shows the tree structure of Iwanami Kokugo Jiten. In this research, we used Annotated Corpus of Iwanami Japanese Dictionary Fifth Edition 2004, which is BCCWJ tagged with Iwamnami Kokugo Jiten, provided Gengo Shigen Kyokai, or Language Resource Academy [6].

3.2. Concept Tags from WLSP

WLSP is a Japanese thesaurus in which a word is classified and ordered according to its meaning. One record is composed of the following elements, record ID number, lemma number, type of record, class, division, section, article, concept number, paragraph number, small paragraph number, word number, lemma with explanatory note, lemma without explanatory note, reading and reverse reading. Concept number consists of a category, a medium item and a classification item. We used concept numbers as the concept tags. For example, "子供 (child or children)" is polyseme and two concepts are registered in WLSP, which are "1.2050" and "1.2130" (Table 2). This paper utilizes a corpus that is in its infancy, namely BCCWJ annotated with concept tags or concept numbers of WLSP.

The goal of our research is to find the correspondences of the meaning tags from two dictionaries. In the example of "子供 (child or children)," we think that the word senses "17877-0-0-1-0" and "17877-0-0-2-0" in Iwanami Kokugo Jiten respectively correspond to concepts "1.2050" and "1.2130" in WLSP, however, please note that the meaning tags do not always correspond one-to-one. We utilized only two sets of meaning tag from BCCWJ and did not use the reference source: the dictionaries.

Figure 2 shows the tree structure of WLSP.

3.3. Bilingual Word Embeddings

We used monolingual mapping. Monolingual mapping consists of two steps. First, monolingual word embeddings are trained for each language. In our research, one language corresponds to one meaning tag set in Japanese. After that, they are mapped to a common vector space so that word embeddings of the words whose meanings are similar to each other in two languages can be brought closer. Because the geometrical relations that hold between words are similar across languages, it is possible to transform a vector space of a language to that of another language using a linear projection. In this research, we adapted two methods of BWE, linear transformation matrix and VecMap. A

---

[2]We eliminated the compound words from the dictionary.

[4]English translations in Table 1 are quoted from Longman Dictionary of Contemporary English [5].

[6]https://www.gsk.or.jp/catalog/gsk2010-a/

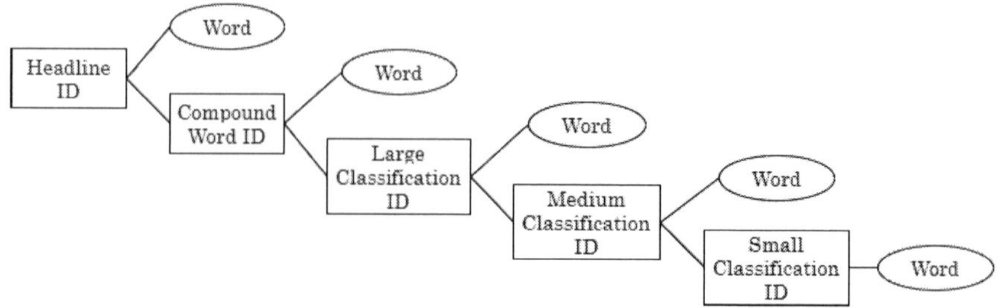

Figure 1: Tree Structure of Iwanami Kokugo Jiten

Table 2: Concept-tags and Their Corresponding Class, Division, Section of "子供 (child or children)" from WLSP

Concept number	Class	Division	Section	Article
1.2050	Nominal words	Agent	Human	Young or old
1.2130	Nominal words	Agent	Family	Child or descendant

linear projection matrix W was learned when we used a linear transformation matrix. VecMap is an implementation of a framework of Artetxe et al. to learn cross-lingual word embedding mappings (Artetxe et al., 2017)(Artetxe et al., 2018a)(Artetxe et al., 2018b).

4. Experiment

4.1. Experimental Setting

We utilized BCCWJ tagged with word senses of Iwanami Kokugo Jiten and BCCWJ tagged with concepts of WLSP. Table 3 shows the number of word tokens, unique words, unique word senses, and unique concepts.

Table 3: Statistic Data of BCCWJ

Number of Word tokens	340,995
Number of Unique Words	25,321
Number of Unique Word Senses	26,713
Number of Unique Concepts	3,164

The settings of word2vec are shown in Table 4. We used C-Bow algorithm and we set the number of dimensions as 200, the window size as 5, the number of iterations as 5, the batch size as 1,000, and the min-count as 1, respectively. We set the min-count as 1 because the corpus size was small.

Table 4: Settings of word2vec

Parameters	Settings
Dimensionality	200
Learning Algorithm	C-BoW
Window Size	5
Number of Epochs	5
Batch Size	1,000
min-count	1

4.1.1. Linear Transformation Matrix

When a linear project matrix is learnt, we conduct experiments as follows.

1. Generate a word-sense-tag and concept-tag corpora respectively, and learn word-sense or concept embeddings for each corpus from them using word2vec [7] (Mikolov et al., 2013a; Mikolov et al., 2013c; Mikolov et al., 2013d) (cf. Figure 3).

2. Learn a linear projection matrix W from the vector space of the word-senses to that of the concepts using pairs of the embeddings for monosemous common nouns, which are generated in the last step.

3. Apply the matrix W to the word-sense embeddings and obtain the projected concept embeddings for them.

We defined a monosemous word as a word that meets two conditions, which are, (1) it has only one sense in Iwanami Kokugo Jiten and (2) it does not have any concept number in WLSP. We chose them because the concepts in WLSP are like synsets in English WordNet; many words share a concept. Therefore, if a word has a concept number, we cannot treat the word as monosemous word because we generated word embeddings for each concept number. We used 104 monosemous common nouns as seed words of our experiments. We randomly extracted ten words for evaluation data and used other 94 words for the training data to obtain the number of epochs that minimize the loss. We iterated this operation for 20 times and used the average number of epochs for the number of epochs of the final experiment.

Table 5 shows learning parameters of the linear transformation matrix.

Table 5: Learning Parameters of Linear Transformation Matrix

Parameters	Settings
Dimensionality	200×200
Optimization Algorithm	Adam
Number of Epochs	118

---

[7] https://code.google.com/archive/p/word2vec/

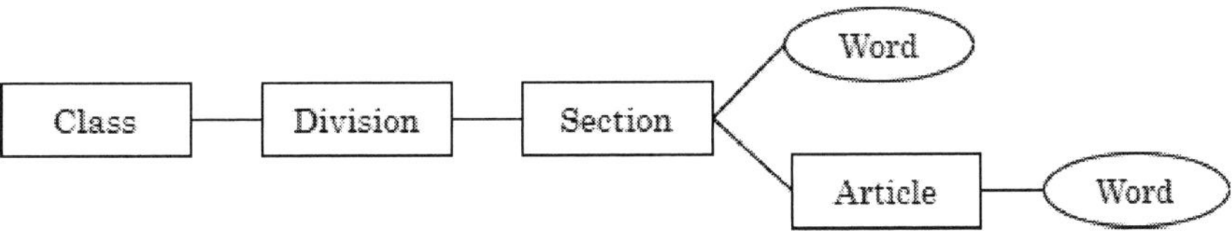

Figure 2: Tree Structure of WLSP

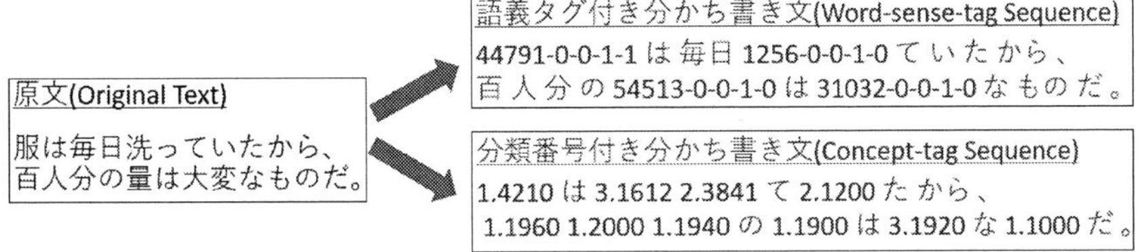

Figure 3: Word-sense-tag and Concept-tag Sentences

4.1.2. VecMap

VecMap [8] is used for the second method of BWE. When we used a linear transformation matrix, we projected the vector space of word senses of Iwanami Kokugo Jiten into that of concepts of WLSP. However, VecMap projects both the vector spaces of word senses and concepts into a new vector space. The three options, supervised, semi-supervised, and identical, were compared. Supervised and semi-supervised VecMap utilize the specified words but Identical VecMap uses identical words in two languages as the seeds of the projection. Therefore, the seed words of supervised and semi-supervised VecMap are the same as the linear transformation matrix but that of identical VecMap is different from it. The seed words of identical VecMap is monosemous words whereas those of supervised or semi-supervised VecMap is monosemous common nouns. The number of monosemous words, the seed words of identical VecMap, is 2,015. We used default settings for the tool of VecMap for each option. Table 6 lists the default settings of the parameters of each specific option and the general default settings of them.

4.1.3. Evaluation

We evaluated the correspondences of the meaning tags as follows.

1. Calculate the cosine similarities between the projected concept embeddings and the embeddings of the concepts from the target word.

2. Choose the concepts that have the highest similarities to the projected concept embeddings as the corresponding concepts for the word senses.

3. Calculate the accuracy.

We targeted at polysemous nouns that appeared equal to or more than 50 times in the corpus. They were nine words, which were, "関係 (relationship)", "技術 (technology)", "現場 (field)", "子供 (child)", "時間 (time) ", "市場 (market)", "電話 (phone)", "場所 (place)", and "前 (before)"

---

[8]https://github.com/artetxem/vecmap#publications

and their word senses were 25 in total. We regarded an estimated concept tag to be correct when it is the same to the tag aligned with its corresponding sense tag most frequently in the tagged corpus. We evaluated the most frequent sense (MFS) accuracy for comparison. For MFS, the most frequent concept from WLSP for each word type in a corpus was regarded as the corresponding concept number for all the word senses for the word from Iwanami Kokugo Jiten. Also, we tested another comparative method, which is "concatenation corpus method;" a concept sequence corpus and a word sense sequence corpus are concatenated, and the concept embeddings and the word sense embeddings were generated together at the same time.

4.2. Results

Table 7 shows the accuracies of the corresponding meanings. Thirteen out of 25 word senses were aligned with the correct concept tags by a linear transformation matrix, and the accuracy was 52.0%. The results of VecMap were 36.0%, 48.0%, and 48.0% when supervised, semi-supervised, and identical options were used. In the comparative experiment, 16 out of 25 word senses were aligned with the correct concept tags by both the MFS and corpus concatenation methods, and the accuracy was 64.0%. The accuracy of the random baseline, which is the method where each word sense was chosen at random, was 41.5%. The list of concept tags estimated by the linear transformation matrix, i.e., the best method of BWE in Table 7, the MFS and corpus concatenation methods, and the oracle for 25 word senses of 9 words are shown in Table 8. The correct concept tags are shown in bold. "X-X-X-X" in the word sense of "前 (before)" means a new word sense not listed in a dictionary, and in this research, it was considered as one of the word sense of the experiment.

5. Discussion

According to Table 7, the accuracies of the proposed the methods were lower than the accuracy of the MFS method and the corpus concatenation method. However, as mentioned above, in reality, one concept tag does not always

Table 6: Parameters of VecMap

Option	Parameter	Default Setting of Specific Option	General Default Setting
Supervised	Batch size	1000	10000
Semi-supervised	Self-Learning	TRUE	FALSE
Semi-supervised	Vocabulary_cutoff	200,000	0
Semi-supervised	csls_neibourhood	10	0
Identical	Self-Learning	TRUE	FALSE
Identical	Vocabulary_cutoff	200,000	0
Identical	csls_neibourhood	10	0

Table 7: Accuracies of Each Method

Method	Accuracy
Linear Transformation Matrix	52.0 %
VecMap Supervised	36.0 %
VecMap Semi-supervised	48.0 %
VecMap Identical	48.0 %
MFS	64.0 %
Corpus Concatenation	64.0 %
Random	41.5 %

correspond one sense tag. Sometimes one concept tag corresponds to plural sense tags and vice versa. We chose to make one-to-one correspondence for simplicity. From this perspective, the proposed methods have an advantage: the relations of the sense tags corresponding to a concept tag can be examined by mapping the sense embeddings to the vector space of the concept tags. Since the corpus concatenation method also uses word2vec, it also examine the relations of the sense tags but our method could be performed when we have only concept or word sense embeddings and do not have any tagged corpora.

Also, in this research, we conducted the experiments using a corpus where two kinds of meaning tags are assigned. However, it is possible to use two different corpora for two meaning tag sets for our proposed methods, the use of BWE. In other words, we can conduct the experiments using two corpora, for example, a corpus assigned with concept tags from WLSP and another corpus assigned with word senses from Iwanami Kokugo Jiten. In that case, comparable corpora would be better than two monolingual corpora for BWE because the meanings of words should be similar to each other. Also, the accuracies may be lower when we use different two corpora because words do not share the contexts in two monolingual corpora. Furthermore, it is desirable to use a relatively large corpus for the experiments in this research because only the concepts or word senses of words appeared in the corpus are able to have a corresponding meaning.

In this research, the experiments were performed on words that appeared 50 times or more in the corpus, but when the number of occurrences for each word sense was counted, there were four word senses that appeared only once. Since we used word2vec tool, it is preferable to use a corpus where all the meanings appear more than the threshold value [9]. We had a hypothesis that relatively large number of examples are required to generate meaning embeddings. Therefore, we examined how the correspondence accuracies between the word senses and the concepts differ depending on the occurrences of the word senses in the corpus. Figure 4 shows correct and incorrect numbers of the examples according to the occurrences of the word senses. For this figure, 25 word senses were grouped by occurrences so that each group has 5 word senses. The numbers of correct and incorrect answers are plotted on the vertical axis for each group and these groups are shown in order of the decreasing occurrences. The label of the bar graph in Figure 4 indicates "minimum number of occurrences in each group" − "maximum number of occurrences in each group".

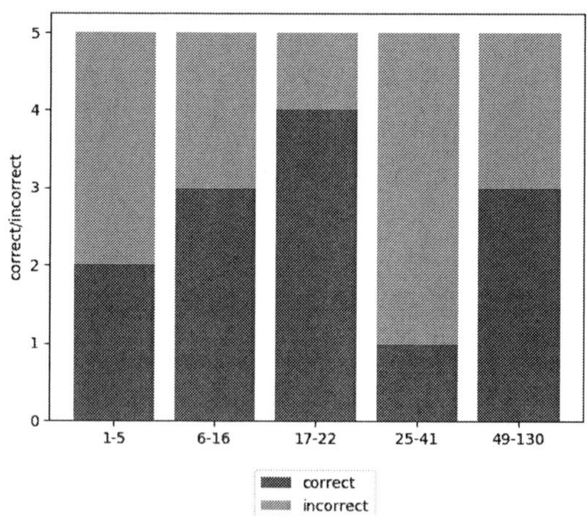

Figure 4: Numbers of correct and incorrect answers according to occurrences of the word senses

Despite our hypothesis, according to Figure 4, there was no correlation between the occurrences of the word senses and the correspondence accuracies in this research.

Because both the concept tags and the word sense tags were manually annotated on BCCWJ, the accuracies of annotations are very high. However, since there are still few corpora with which two or more types of tags are assigned, we plan to use a tagger to automatically tag one type of meaning tags on a corpus with another type of meaning tags for the preprocessing of the proposed method for future work. However, in this case, the performance of the

---

[9]Word2vec generates vectors only for the word (word senses or concepts in this research) that appeared equal to or more than a threshold value. Default setting is five. We set this value to one to acquire meaning vectors for the words that appeared only once.

Table 8: Correspondence Table of "Iwanami Kokugo Jiten" and "WLSP"

Words	Word Numbers	Word Senses	Concept Numbers			
			Linear transformation Matrix	MFS	Corpus Concatenation	Oracle
関係 (relationship)	9667	0-0-1-0	**1.1110**	**1.1110**	**1.1110**	1.1110
		0-0-2-0	1.3500	**1.1110**	**1.1110**	1.1110
		0-0-3-0	**1.1110**	**1.1110**	**1.1110**	1.1110
技術 (technology)	10703	0-0-1-0	1.3421	**1.3850**	**1.3850**	1.3850
		0-0-2-0	**1.3421**	1.3850	1.3850	1.3421
現場 (field)	15615	0-0-1-0	1.2620	1.2620	**1.1700**	1.1700
		0-0-2-0	**1.2620**	**1.2620**	**1.2620**	1.2620
子供 (child)	17877	0-0-1-0	1.2130	**1.2050**	1.2130	1.2050
		0-0-2-0	**1.2130**	1.2050	**1.2130**	1.2130
時間 (time)	20676	0-0-1-0	**1.1600**	**1.1600**	1.1962	1.1600
		0-0-2-0	**1.1962**	1.1600	**1.1962**	1.1962
		0-0-3-0	**1.1600**	**1.1600**	**1.1600**	1.1600
		0-0-4-0	1.1962	**1.1600**	**1.1600**	1.1600
市場 (market)	21128	0-0-1-0	1.2600	1.2600	**1.2640**	1.2640
		0-0-2-0	**1.2600**	**1.2600**	1.2640	1.2600
		0-0-3-0	**1.2600**	**1.2600**	1.2640	1.2600
電話 (phone)	35881	0-0-1-0	1.4620	**1.3122**	**1.3122**	1.3122
		0-0-2-0	**1.4620**	1.3122	**1.4620**	1.4620
場所 (place)	41150	0-0-1-0	1.3833	**1.1700**	**1.1700**	1.1700
		0-0-2-0	1.3833	**1.1700**	1.3833	1.1700
前 (before)	48488	0-0-1-1	**1.1740**	1.1670	**1.1740**	1.1740
		0-0-2-0	1.1650	1.1670	**1.1740**	1.1740
		0-0-2-1	1.1635	**1.1670**	1.1635	1.1670
		0-0-2-2	1.1635	**1.1670**	1.1740	1.1670
		X-X-X-X	**1.1635**	1.1670	1.1650	1.1635

tagger should be considered to guarantee the quality of the automatic tagged corpus.

6. Conclusion

In this research, we described how to utilize bilingual word embeddings to obtain the correspondences of meanigs from two dictionaries in one language and investigated the effectiveness of the method. We used BCCWJ with concept tags from WLSP and sense tags from Iwanami Kokugo Jiten for the experiments. The experiments showed that the correspondence accuracies of the proposed methods were lower than MFS baseline or the corpus concatenation method. However, because our method utilizes the embedding vectors of the word senses, the relation of the sense tags corresponding to concept tags can be examined by mapping the sense embeddings to the vector space of the concept tags. Also, our method could be performed when we have only concept or word sense embeddings. However, it is necessary to expand the corpus for the further evaluation because the proposed method uses one corpus for both the training and the test and only the word senses or the concepts that appeared in the corpus are able to have correspondence. In addition, we would like to investigate further how the accuracy of this study changes when the corpus is expanded.

Acknowledgements

This work was supported by JSPS KAKENHI Grants Number 18K11421, 17H00917, and a project of the Center for Corpus Development, NINJAL.

References

Artetxe, M., Labaka, G., and Agirre, E. (2017). Learning bilingual word embeddings with (almost) no bilingual data. In *Proceedings of the 55th Annual Meeting of the Association for Computational Linguistics (Volume 1: Long Papers)*, pages 451–462.

Artetxe, M., Labaka, G., and Agirre, E. (2018a). Generalizing and improving bilingual word embedding mappings with a multi-step framework of linear transformations. In *Proceedings of the Thirty-Second AAAI Conference on Artificial Intelligence*, pages 5012–5019.

Artetxe, M., Labaka, G., and Agirre, E. (2018b). A robust self-learning method for fully unsupervised crosslingual mappings of word embeddings. In *Proceedings of the 56th Annual Meeting of the Association for Computational Linguistics (Volume 1: Long Papers)*, pages 789–798.

Hermann, K. M. and Blunsom, P. (2014). Multilingual models for compositional distributed semantics. *arXiv preprint arXiv:1404.4641*.

Klementiev, A., Titov, I., and Bhattarai, B. (2012). Inducing crosslingual distributed representations of words. *Proceedings of COLING 2012*, pages 1459–1474.

Maekawa, K., Yamazaki, M., Ogiso, T., Maruyama, T., Ogura, H., Kashino, W., Koiso, H., Yamaguchi, M., Tanaka, M., and Den, Y. (2014). Balanced corpus of contemporary written japanese. *Language resources and evaluation*, 48(2):345–371.

Mikolov, T., Chen, K., Corrado, G., and Dean, J. (2013a). Efficient estimation of word representations in vector space. In *Proceedings of ICLR Workshop 2013*, pages 1–12.

Mikolov, T., Le, Q. V., and Sutskever, I. (2013b). Exploiting similarities among languages for machine translation. *arXiv preprint arXiv:1309.4168*.

Mikolov, T., Sutskever, I., Chen, K., Corrado, G., and Dean, J. (2013c). Distributed representations of words and phrases and their compositionality. In *Proceedings of NIPS 2013*, pages 1–9.

Mikolov, T., tau Yih, W., and Zweig, G. (2013d). Linguistic regularities in continuous space word representations. In *Proceedings of NAACL 2013*, pages 746–751.

National Institute for Japanese Language and Linguistics. (1964). *Word List by Semantic Principles*. Shuuei Shuppan, In Japanese.

Nishio, M., Iwabuchi, E., and Mizutani, S. (1994). *Iwanami Kokugo Jiten Dai Go Han*. Iwanami Publisher, In Japanese.

Wu, P., Kondo, M., Moriyama, N., Ogiwara, A., and Asahara, M. (2019). Alignment table between 'word list by semantic principles' and 'annotated corpus of iwanami japanese dictionary fifth edition 2004'. In *Proceedings of the Language Resources Workshop 2019*, pages 337–342.

Xiao, M. and Guo, Y. (2014). Distributed word representation learning for cross-lingual dependency parsing. In *Proceedings of the Eighteenth Conference on Computational Natural Language Learning*, pages 119–129.

Zou, W. Y., Socher, R., Cer, D., and Manning, C. D. (2013). Bilingual word embeddings for phrase-based machine translation. In *Proceedings of the 2013 Conference on Empirical Methods in Natural Language Processing*, pages 1393–1398.

Proceedings of the 13th Workshop on Building and Using Comparable Corpora, pages 29–34
Language Resources and Evaluation Conference (LREC 2020), Marseille, 11–16 May 2020
© European Language Resources Association (ELRA), licensed under CC-BY-NC

Mining Semantic Relations from Comparable Corpora through Intersections of Word Embeddings

Špela Vintar[1], Larisa Grčić Simeunović[2], Matej Martinc[3], Senja Pollak[4], Uroš Stepišnik[5]
University of Ljubljana[1,5], University of Zadar[2], Jožef Stefan Institute[3,4]
Aškerčeva 2, SI-1000 Ljubljana, M. Pavlinovića 1, HR-23000 Zadar, Jamova cesta 39, SI-1000 Ljubljana
spela.vintar@ff.uni-lj.si, lgrcic@unizd.hr, matej.martinc@ijs.si, senja.pollak@ijs.si, uros.stepisnik@ff.uni-lj.si

Abstract

We report an experiment aimed at extracting words expressing a specific semantic relation using intersections of word embeddings. In a multilingual frame-based domain model, specific features of a concept are typically described through a set of non-arbitrary semantic relations. In karstology, our domain of choice which we are exploring though a comparable corpus in English and Croatian, karst phenomena such as landforms are usually described through their FORM, LOCATION, CAUSE, FUNCTION and COMPOSITION. We propose an approach to mine words pertaining to each of these relations by using a small number of seed adjectives, for which we retrieve closest words using word embeddings and then use intersections of these neighbourhoods to refine our search. Such cross-language expansion of semantically-rich vocabulary is a valuable aid in improving the coverage of a multilingual knowledge base, but also in exploring differences between languages in their respective conceptualisations of the domain.

Keywords : semantic relations, word embeddings, comparable corpus, karstology, frame-based terminology

1. Introduction

The frame-based approach in terminology (FBT; Faber, 2012; Faber, 2015; Faber & Cabezas-García, 2019) has brought the notion that specialised knowledge can be modelled through conceptual frames which simulate the cognitive patterns in our minds. According to Faber (2012), "[a] frame is thus as an organized package of knowledge that humans retrieve from long-term memory to make sense of the world." Two of the most significant practical contributions of FBT are on the one hand the consolidation between the conceptual and the textual level of domain representation by using specialised corpora for the induction of frames or event templates, and on the other hand the realisation that such frames and templates are not universal but contextually, culturally and linguistically bound.

On a more practical level, the frame-based approach to domain modelling fosters a dynamic and process-oriented view of the concepts, actions, properties and events leading to a deeper understanding of the domain. This is particularly relevant for a domain such as karstology where karst landscapes and landforms are the result of complex and prolonged natural processes occurring in specific environments and under specific sets of conditions.

The broader context for this research is the TermFrame project which employs and extends the frame-based approach to build a visual knowledge base for the domain of karstology in three languages, English, Slovene and Croatian; as well as explores new methods of knowledge extraction from specialized texts (Vintar et al., 2019, Miljkovic et al., 2019, Pollak et al. 2019).

The domain of karstology is conceptualized in terms of events where natural or human agents initiate actions or processes which affect patients in specific ways and thus result in various karst features. In order to explore typical conceptual frames in karstology we devised a domain-specific concept hierarchy of semantic categories, and each category can be described by a set of relations which reveal its typical features. For example, the category of *surface landforms* is typically described by relations that express form, size, location and cause while concepts from the category of *hydrological landforms* are usually defined by the relations cause, location and function.

When building a multilingual knowledge base, identifying such relations is important from the perspective of organising knowledge and ensuring maximum coverage of the domain. For example, COMPOSITION in terms of geological structure plays a crucial role in karstology because karst phenomena can only develop on soluble rocks. It is therefore extremely useful if we can access the entire inventory of expressions denoting COMPOSITION in our corpus, and also compare them between languages as this gives important clues about the domain itself, e.g. the prominence of certain minerals in different geographical regions.

In this research we propose a method to extract expressions pertaining to a specific semantic relation from a comparable English and Croatian corpus by providing a limited number of seed words for each language and relation, then using word embeddings to identify words belonging to same relation class. The seed words in our study are limited to adjectives because of their combinatorial potential within multi-word terms and the observation that semantic relations are frequently expressed through adjectives.

2. Related work

One of the aims of this study is to leverage word embeddings and a set of seed adjectives expressing semantic relations in order to extract additional adjectives that express the same semantic relation/attribute. This is in essence a set expansion task and previous research on a related subject was conducted by Diaz et al. (2016), who showed that embeddings can be employed for query expansion on domain specific texts. The research concludes that due to strong language use variation in specialized corpora, domain specific embeddings (trained locally on a small specialized corpora) outperform non-topic specific general embeddings trained on a much larger general corpus. A very similar approach for set expansion in the domain of karstology was employed by Pollak et al. (2019) for the purposes of extending terminology.

Previous authors (Duran Muñoz, 2019, Bhat, 1994, Wierzbicka, 1986, Fellbaum et al., 1993, L'Homme, 2002) have already examined the role of adjectives in specialised languages and confirmed their importance in expressing key properties of specialized concepts as well as appearing as parts of multi-word terms. A particularly relevant analysis of semantic relations in complex nominals was performed by Cabezas-García and León-Araúz (2018), who use knowledge patterns and verb paraphrases to construct a frame-based model of semantic categories and the semantic relations occurring between them. They show that a particular combinatorial pattern established for a set of nouns can be extrapolated to the entire semantic category and potentially used for relation induction.

We are also aware of several studies describing the semantic representation of adjectives in ontologies for other domains, e.g. legal (Bertoldi and Chisman, 2007), environment (Campos Alonso and Castells Torner, 2010), plant morphology (Pitkanen-Heikkila, 2015) and waste management (Altmanova et al., 2018).

3. Karstology and the TermFrame Corpus

Karstology is the study of karst, a type of landscape developing on soluble rocks such as limestone, marble or gypsum. Its most prominent features include caves, various types of relief depressions, conical hills, springs, ponors and similar. It is an interdisciplinary domain partly overlapping with surface and subsurface geomorphology, geology, hydrology and other fields.

For the purposes of our research, we used the English and Croatian parts of the TermFrame corpus, which otherwise also contains Slovene as the third language. The comparable corpus contains relevant contemporary works on karstology and is representative in terms of the domain and text types included. It comprises scientific papers, books, articles, doctoral and master's theses, glossaries and textbooks. Table 1 gives basic information about the corpus.

	English	Croatian
Tokens	2,721,042	1,229,368
Words	2,195,982	969,735
Sentences	97,187	53,017
Documents	57	43

Table 1: Corpus information

4. Methods

4.1 Framing karstology

The TermFrame project models the karstology domain using a hierarchy of semantic categories and a set of relations which allow us to describe and model karst events (Vintar et al., 2019). According to the geomorphologic analytical approach (Pavlopoulos et al., 2009), the relations describe different aspects of concepts, such as spatial distribution (HAS_LOCATION; HAS_POSITION), morphography (HAS_FORM; CONTAINS), morphometry (HAS_SIZE), morphostructure (COMPOSED_OF), morphogenesis (HAS_CAUSE), morphodynamics (AFFECTS; HAS_RESULT; HAS_FUNCTION), and morphochronology (OCCURS_IN_TIME). Additional relations were applied for general properties (HAS_ATTRIBUTE; DEFINED_AS), and for research methods (STUDIES; MEASURES).

The research described here focuses on the 5 relations which occur most frequently in the definitions of karst landforms and processes, and they also govern the formation of multi-word terms as illustrated by examples below.

underground cave ⇒ LOCATION (cave) = underground

fluvial sediment ⇒ CAUSE (sediment)=fluvial

enclosed depression ⇒ FORM (depression)= enclosed

gypsum karst ⇒ COMPOSITION (karst)=gypsum

soluble rock ⇒ FUNCTION (rock)=soluble

We thus examined the contexts expressing the selected relations in the TermFrame corpus of annotated definitions (Vintar et al., 2019). From these contexts we obtained lists of seed adjectives for each relation and both languages, which were validated by a domain expert:

LOCATION
English*: coastal, littoral, sublittoral, submarine, oceanic, subsurface, subterranean, subterraneous, subaerial, underground, aquatic, subaqueous, internal, subglacial, epigenic, phreatic, vadose, epiphreatic*

Croatian*: obalni, litoralan, priobalni, podmorski, oceanski, podzeman, freatski, vadozan, podvodan, dolinski, špiljski, epifreatski*

CAUSE
English: fluvial, allogenic, tectonic, erosional, alluvial, volcanic, lacustrine, solutional, aeolian, periglacial, anthropogenic

Croatian: fluvijalni, alogeni, tektonski, erozijski, aluvijalan, vulkanski, lakustrijski, eolski, periglacijalni, antropogeni

FORM
English: *polygonal, vertical, dendritic, shallow, enclosed, elongated, flat, steep, cavernicolous, detrital*

Croatian: vertikalan, ravnocrtan, strm, kavernozan, horizontalan, mrežast, longitudinalan, kružan, razgranat, ulegnut, uravnjen

COMPOSITION
English: *carbonate, limestone, dolomitic, sedimentary, sulfate, calcareous, carboniferous, silicate, sulfuric, diagenetic, siliceous, clay, volcanoclastic*

Croatian: karbonatni, vapnenački, dolomitski, sedimentan, sulfatni, kalcitan, karbonski, sulfatni, glinovit, sedreni, stijenski,klastičan,sedreni

FUNCTION
English: impermeable, permeable, solutional, hydrothermal, speleological, geological, soluble, porous, depositional, regressive, undersaturated

Croatian: nepropustan, propustan, speleološki, geološki, topiv, porozan, taložan, urušan

4.2   Word embeddings

Our initial assumption was that the word embeddings of a set of adjectives expressing a specific semantic relation, such as CAUSE, FORM or COMPOSITION, share a certain semantic component which can be used to extract other adjectives expressing the same relation.

To test this assumption, we first train FastText embeddings (Bojanowski et al., 2017) on the English and the Croatian part of the TermFrame corpus respectively (see Section 3). Embeddings were calculated for all the words that appear in the corpus at least three times and we use a skip-gram model with an embedding dimension of 100. For each seed adjective expressing a specific semantic relation, we use embeddings to find a set of 100 closest words according to the cosine distance. In order to find words of similar semantic provenance that express a specific semantic relation, in the next step we calculate all non-empty intersections between these sets of 100 closest words for all possible subsets of a set of adjectives for each relation. These subsets range in size from 10 to 2, since 10 is the largest subset of seed adjectives for a relation, for which a non-empty intersection was returned. All words found in these intersections are retained as candidate words that express a specific relation and are used in manual evaluation (see Section 5). For example, (see examples (1) and (2) below), the intersection of the closest embeddings for a subset of 5 English input words for LOCATION (*coastal, littoral, oceanic, submarine, subterranean*) yields the single word *nonmarine* as intersection, while the intersection for the subset of 3 Croatian input words for FORM (*horizontalan, kružan, vertikalan*) yields 8 words in the intersection:

(1)   SIZE: 5
      SUBSET: coastal, littoral, oceanic, submarine, subterranean INTERSECTION: nonmarine
(2)   SIZE: 3   SUBSET: horizontalan, kružan, vertikalan   INTERSECTION: okomito, sjecište, vodoravan, inverzan, okomit, nepravilan, presjecište, konveksan

5.   Results and Discussion

Intersections were computed for subsets of input words ranging from maximum 10 to 2 words, whereby most intersections were empty for larger subsets and only started yielding results from size 7 downwards (see Table 2).

Our first observation is that both in English and Croatian a large majority of extracted words are adjectives and other words functioning as premodifiers in multi-word terms, thus illustrating that the embeddings capture also syntactic properties.

Since the overall goal of the experiment is to extract words pertaining to the same semantic relation, we first report the total number of extracted words and the number of correctly predicted ones, i.e. belonging to the same semantic class as the input words (Table 2).

	location		function		form		composition		cause	
	en	cr	en	cr	en	cr	en	cr	en	cr
N	357	228	147	152	164	152	293	244	183	181
C	118	88	68	43	108	97	184	197	88	132
P	0.33	0.39	0.46	0.28	0.66	0.64	0.63	0.80	0.48	0.73

Table 2: Precision per semantic relation and language (N = number of extracted words, C = correct, P = precision (C/N))

A quick glance at Table 2 shows that the numbers of extracted words are slightly lower for Croatian, which is possibly due to the difference in the size of corpora, but the overall lowest and highest precisions are also found for Croatian candidates. Next we observe large differences between individual semantic relations, both in terms of precision of prediction and the yield, but relatively similar performance across both languages. The largest number of correctly extracted candidates is achieved for COMPOSITION, where an input of only 13 words allows us to extract 184 English and 197 Croatian expressions for geological or chemical composition, e.g. *lithoclast, calcitic, azurite, loessic, gneiss, chalky, magmatic, pyrite, framestone, siliclastic* and *kalkarenit, laporovit, škriljac, glinenac, piroksenit, fliški* etc. Many of the extracted expressions are highly specialised and occur in the corpus with a very low frequency, yet their membership in the semantic class could still be correctly predicted.

On the other hand, the LOCATION relation is more difficult to capture because it may refer to the position of an entity within the karst system, its position relative to some other entity or its position relative to the land or sea. The retrieved words include many geographical names, e.g. *Baltic, Bahamian;kvarnerski, mosorski,* which we do not count as positives for the simple reason that our annotation scheme uses a different semantic relation (HAS_POSITION) for toponyms.

Next, we measure the precision of the predicted relation for each intersection, and we report average precision for each subset size and each language (see Table 3 and Table 4). We use precision@M denoting the number of true predictions divided by the number of all words in the intersection, and precision@5 where the size of the intersection is fixed to 5 words. In this case, a perfect precision is not possible for intersections containing less than 5 words and intersections containing more than 5 words are truncated. For the example (1) above, precision@M = 1 and precision@5 = 0.2.

As mentioned before, most intersections for larger subsets (English 8-10 input words, Croatian 7-10 input words) were empty, except for COMPOSITION in English. This would indicate that the most suitable subset size ranges from 2 to 6 input words. In English, poorest results were obtained for FUNCTION, where the intersections of subsets 4-6 contained only a single word (*sluggish*), which expresses manner of (water) movement but not function. Results for FORM, COMPOSITION and CAUSE were however promising in that they yielded highly accurate predictions, e.g. *zigzag, honeycomb, steep, curvilinear, elliptical, coalescent, sharp, semicircular, asymmetric, sinusoidal, pinnacled, undulating* for FORM and *compressional, geogenic, preglacial, bioclastic, erosional, disolutional, orogenic, tensional* etc. for CAUSE.

subset size	location		function		form		composition		cause	
	p@M	p@5	p@M	p@5	p@M	p@5	p@M	p@5	p@M	p@5
10							1	0.20		
9							1	0.20		
8							1	0.21		
7	0	0					0.99	0.24	1	0.20
6	0.36	0.07	0	0	1	0.2	0.98	0.28	0.78	0.16
5	0.45	0.13	0	0	1	0.22	0.95	0.35	0.65	0.16
4	0.45	0.17	0.01	0	1	0.31	0.91	0.44	0.60	0.20
3	0.42	0.22	0.10	0.03	0.94	0.47	0.85	0.53	0.60	0.30
2	0.37	0.29	0.26	0.13	0.70	0.55	0.75	0.59	0.56	0.39

Table 3: Precision of English predicted words per subset size

subset size	location		function		form		composition		cause	
	p@M	p@5	p@M	p@5	p@M	p@5	p@M	p@5	p@M	p@5
6	0	0								
5	0	0	0.33	0.20	1	0.20	0	0	0.50	0.10
4	0.10	0.05	0.33	0.28	0.92	0.20	0.69	0.20	0.53	0.15
3	0.28	0.16	0.32	0.30	0.78	0.28	0.79	0.35	0.65	0.27
2	0.33	0.30	0.32	0.20	0.72	0.49	0.79	0.62	0.72	0.55

Table 4: Precision of Croatian predicted words per subset size

FUNCTION also had the lowest yield of meaningful expressions in Croatian, with only one non-empty intersection for subset 5, but on the other hand the entire range of karst-related studies was retrieved by intersecting *geološki* and *speleološki (3)*:

(3) SIZE: 2
    SUBSET: geološki, speleološki
    INTERSECTION: arheološki, biospeleološki, geomofološki, tipološki, geoekološki, biološki, mitološki, kršološki, ontološki, geoekološka, aerološki, fiziološki, paleokrški, speleomorfološki, drološki, geokronološki, etnološki, paleontološki, filološki

Results for English also show a positive linear correlation between the subset size and precision@M (especially for the relations FORM, COMPOSITION AND CAUSE), and a negative linear correlation between the subset size and precision@5. This phenomenon can be explained with the fact that at large subset sizes there are less than five words in the intersection which has a negative impact on precision@5, but as the few extracted examples are likely to be correct, it has a positive impact on precision@M. On the other hand, at small subset sizes the number of words in the intersection will increase, which has a positive effect on precision@5 but also negatively affects precision@M, since the percentage of correctly retrieved words in the intersection decreases. The results for Croatian also show a strong negative linear correlation between the subset size and precision@5, while for precison@M the correlation somewhat varies between relations, ranging from being negative for LOCATION, CAUSE and COMPOSITION, to no correlation for FUNCTION, and to a positive correlation for the FORM relation. This means that for Croatian a larger subset size does not necessarily guarantee that a larger percentage of extracted examples will be correct.

To understand why relations perform differently in such an experimental setting we must consider their conceptual role within the frame-based domain model. It is clear that there can be an almost indefinite number of words used to describe the form of an entity in the karst landscape - think just of the multitude of underground forms found in caves. The embeddings thus successfully capture about one hundred expressions for FORM in each language, yet miss words like *ravničast, ponikvast, kavernozan, terasast, klifast, zaravnjen* etc. On the other hand, not all karst landforms have functions in the karstologic event, and the number of possible causes is also limited. For CAUSE, certain suffixes seem especially productive and allow us to extract relevant expressions – often cognates – on this basis: -genic/-gen, -genijski, -genski (*epigenic, geogenic, cryogenic, orogenic, biogenic, pathogenic, hypogenic, glacigenic, rheogenic / epigenijski, orogenski, egzogen, kemogen, zoogen, biogen, kriogen*); -glacial/-glacijalan (*preglacial, subglacial, fluvioglacial, englacial, proglacial, supraglacial / glacijalan, proglacijalan, interglacijalan, postglacijalan, fluvioglacijalan, periglacijalan*), -luvial/-luvijalan (*alluvial, eluvial, colluvial, pluvial, deluvial / iluvijalan, proluvijalan, delovijalan, diluvijalan, koluvijalan*).

In all experiments reported above we measure precision but not recall. To measure recall we would need to have a list of true positives for each relation, which could only be created manually by inspecting, for instance, all adjectives in the corpus and labelling them with relations, which has not been done as yet.

Finally, during evaluation we noted several ambiguous examples which in some contexts could refer to causes, while in others they denote composition, function or form. For Croatian, some overlap was found between the lists of expressions denoting COMPOSITION and FUNCTION (e.g. *vodopropusan* [permeable]), and for English between COMPOSITION and CAUSE (e.g. *magmatic, sediment, igneous*). Indeed such cases show that some relations are closer than others, and that specialised vocabulary is inherently multidimensional and context-dependent.

6. Conclusions

We explore semantic relations in a comparable English and Croatian corpus of karstology focusing on the adjectives and other premodifiers in multi-word terms. By assuming the frame-based domain model we identify groups of seed adjectives according to the semantic relation they express in the multi-word terms (e.g. FORM, LOCATION, FUNCTION), whereby the conceptual frame provides guidance as to which relations are expected for each concept category.

Against these background assumptions we attempt to extract attributes pertaining to the same relation using word embeddings computed on the two domain-specific corpora. We use subsets of seed adjectives as input and intersect their closest neighbours to extract candidate English and Croatian words.

Results are relatively similar across the two languages, but show high variability in precision between relations, with poor performance for the FUNCTION relation and slightly better for LOCATION. On the other hand, for the other three relations (COMPOSITION, FORM, CAUSE) results seem highly promising in that for both languages the intersections yield relevant candidates with high precision, despite the relatively small size of the domain-specific corpora. Our approach illustrates that word embeddings trained on small specialised corpora can be used to predict the semantic relations in a frame-based setting.

As future work we plan to explore the possibility of modelling karstological processes and events using analogies between semantically related pairs of concepts. It appears that the cognitive dimensions of frame-based knowledge modelling have interesting parallels within the spatial logic of word embeddings.

It is also possible to imagine a scenario where word embeddings and intersections of related words can be used to develop a frame-based model for a new domain, or more specifically to help discern the relations.

Another line of future work will consider cross-lingual query expansion, where we will try to extract adjectives expressing a specific relation in the target language by using only seed terms from the source language. In order to do this we would first need to align embeddings for both languages into a common vector space by using one of the existing methods, e.g., the one proposed in Conneau et. al (2017) that also employs FastText embeddings. Leveraging this procedure we would be able to expand the set of adjectives in a target language with terms that are not clearly associated with the target language seed terms but do however express the same relation.

7. Acknowledgements

This work is supported by the Slovenian Research Agency grant J6-9372 TermFrame: Terminology and knowledge frames across languages, 2018-2021 and by European Union's Horizon 2020 research and innovation programme under grant agreement No. 825153, project EMBEDDIA (Cross-Lingual Embeddings for Less-Represented Languages in European News Media).

8. Bibliographical References

Altmanova, J., Grimaldi, C., Zollo, S. D. (2018). Le rôle des adjectifs dans la catégorisation des déchets. In F. Neveu, B. Harmegnies, L. Hriba et S. Prévost (Eds.), *SHS Web Conferences* 46, 6ème Congrès Mondial de Linguistique Française. Université de Mons, Belgique, pp. 1-15.

Bhat, D.N.S. (1994). The adjectival category: Criteria for differentiation and identification. Amsterdam: John Benjamins Publishing Co.

Bertoldi, A., Chishman, R.L. (2007). Improving Legal Ontologies through Semantic Representation of Adjectives. ICSC 2007, pp. 767-774.

Bojanowski, P. et al. (2017) Enriching word vectors with subword information. *Transactions of the Association for Computational Linguistics* 5, pp: 135-146.

Cabezas-García, M., and León-Araúz, P. (2018). Towards the inference of semantic relations in complex nominals: A pilot study. In Proceedings of the Eleventh International Conference on Language Resources and Evaluation (LREC 2018), pp. 2511-2518.

Campos, Alonso, A. and Castells, Torner S. (2010) Adjectives and collocations in specialized texts: lexicographical implications. In A. Dykstra, T. Schoonheim (Eds.), Proceedings of the XIV EURALEX International Congress. Leeuwarden/Ljouwert: Fryske Akademy - Afûk. pp. 872-881.

Conneau, A., Lample, G., Ranzato, M. A., Denoyer, L. and Jégou, H. (2017). Word translation without parallel data. *arXiv preprint arXiv:1710.04087.*

Diaz, F., Bhaskar M., Craswell, N. (2016). Query expansion with locally-trained word embeddings. *arXiv preprint arXiv:1605.07891*

Durán-Muñoz, I. (2019/forthcoming). Adjectives and their Keyness. A Corpus-based Analysis in English Tourism. *Corpora*, 14 (3). Edinburgh University Press.

Faber, P. (Ed.), (2012). A Cognitive Linguistics View of Terminology and Specialized Language. Berlin and New York: Mouton De Gruyter.

Faber, P. (2015). Frames as a framework for terminology. In Kockaert, H.J., Steurs, F. (Eds) *Handbook of Terminology.* Vol 1. Amsterdam and Philadelphia: John Benjamins, pp. 14-33.

Faber, P., Cabezas-García, M. (2019) Specialized Knowledge Representation: From Terms to Frames. *Research in Language*, 17(2): 197-211.

Fellbaum, C., Gross, D., Miller, K. (1993). Adjectives in WordNet. In G. Miller et al. (Eds.) Five Papers on WordNet. Tehnical Report 43, Cognitive Science Laboratory, Princeton University, pp. 26-39.

L'Homme, M.C. (2002). What can Verbs and Adjectives Tell us about Terms? Paper presented at TKE 2002, Nancy, France.

Miljković, D., Kralj, J., Stepišnik, U., Pollak, S. (2019). Communities of related terms in a karst terminology co-occurrence network. *Proceedings of eLex19*, Sintra, Portugal. pp. 357-373.

Pavlopoulos, K., Evelpidou, N., Vassilopoulos, A. (2009). *Mapping Geomorphological Environments.* Springer, Berlin Heidelberg.

Pitkänen-Heikkilä, K. (2015) Adjectives as terms. *Terminology*, 21 (1):76-101

Pollak, S., Repar, A., Martinc, M., Podpečan, V. (2019). Karst exploration: extracting terms and definitions from karst domain corpus. *Proceedings of eLex19*, Sintra, Portugal. pp. 934-956.

Vintar, Š., Saksida, A., Vrtovec, K., Stepišnik, U. (2019). Modelling specialized knowledge with conceptual frames: the TermFrame approach to a structured visual domain representation. *Proceedings of eLex19*, Sintra, Portugal. pp. 305-318.

Wierzbicka A. (1986) What's in a noun? (Or: How do nouns differ in meaning from adjectives?) *Studies in Language* 10:353-389.

Proceedings of the 13th Workshop on Building and Using Comparable Corpora, pages 35–43
Language Resources and Evaluation Conference (LREC 2020), Marseille, 11–16 May 2020

Benchmarking Multidomain English-Indonesian Machine Translation

Tri Wahyu Guntara[1,2], Alham Fikri Aji[1,3], Radityo Eko Prasojo[1,4]
[1]Kata.ai, Jl. Kemang Raya No. 54, Jakarta, Indonesia
[2]University of Indonesia, Kampus UI Depok, Indonesia
[3]University of Edinburgh, Scotland
[4]Free University of Bolzano, Piazza Domenicani 3, {guntara, aji, ridho}@kata.ai

Abstract

In the context of Machine Translation (MT) from-and-to English, Bahasa Indonesia has been considered a low-resource language, and therefore applying Neural Machine Translation (NMT) which typically requires large training dataset proves to be problematic. In this paper, we show otherwise by collecting large, publicly-available datasets from the Web, which we split into several domains: news, religion, general, and conversation, to train and benchmark some variants of transformer-based NMT models across the domains. We show using BLEU that our models perform well across them and perform comparably with Google Translate. Our datasets (with the standard split for training, validation, and testing), code, and models are available on https://github.com/gunnxx/indonesian-mt-data.
Keywords: Neural machine translation, parallel corpus, English-Indonesian, Indonesian

1. Introduction

With approximately 200 million active speakers, Indonesian (*Bahasa Indonesia*) is the 10th most spoken language in the world (Eberhard et al., 2019). Yet, it is still considered to be one of the under-developed languages. Research in Indonesian Natural Language Processing (NLP) in general has suffered from a lack of open data, standardized benchmark, and reproducible code. Recent work in English-Indonesian (En-Id) machine translation (MT), in particular, has either used (1) closed data (Shahih and Purwarianti, 2016; Octoviani et al., 2019) or (2) open data with unpublished split for training, validation, and testing (Hermanto et al., 2015). Also, mostly only rule-based approaches or Statistical Machine Translation (SMT) were applied (Shahih and Purwarianti, 2016; Octoviani et al., 2019), whereas newer techniques such as Neural Machine Translation (NMT) based on the state-of-the-art Transformer architecture (Vaswani et al., 2017), which has been shown to outperform previous architectures such as the Recurrent Neural Network (RNN) in terms of training time and translation accuracy, has not been utilized. Hermanto et al. (2015) trained an RNN En-Id translation model. However, their model was trained only on a small amount of data with less than 24,000 parallel sentences. Furthermore, all these approaches have been evaluated using different datasets, and so it is unclear how well they perform in comparison to each other.

With the rise of the data-hungry NMT, effort such as the OPUS data portal (Tiedemann, 2012), OpenSubtitles (Lison et al., 2018), and Wikimatrix (Schwenk et al., 2019), has been made to publish more and more parallel data, including English-Indonesian to the number of millions of pairs. However, to the best of our knowledge, there has been no published work that utilizes the data for English-Indonesian machine translation. Therefore, in this particular context, it is currently unclear how useful the data is.

Bahasa Indonesia is a standardized register of Malay and is adopted as the country's national language to unify the archipelago with more than 700 indigenous local languages (Riza, 2008). Consequently, the daily-spoken col-

loquial Indonesian is vastly different from the standardized form due to the influences of the local language and, additionally, some popular foreign languages, such as English or Arabic. This phenomenon affects certain domains, such as the conversational domain where the colloquial Indonesian is typically used more, or the religion domain where Arabic words or phrases are sometimes used "as is" instead of being translated. Recent En-Id MT approaches have not yet considered different domains in Bahasa Indonesia (Shahih and Purwarianti, 2016; Octoviani et al., 2019) and instead have focused more on the news domain, which mostly used the standardized Indonesian (Hermanto et al., 2015).

In this work, our goal is to address the above problems by proposing several contributions as follow:

1. We collect scattered English-Indonesian parallel data available on the Web and divide them into several domains: news, religion, general, and conversation.
2. We introduce new datasets for news and conversation domains by aligning parallel articles and video captions.
3. For each domain, we set a standard data split for training, development, and testing. We further analyze the quality and characteristics of each dataset and each domain.
4. We train several transformer-based NMT models. We perform cross-domain testing to gain some insight into model robustness under domain changes. We conduct a manual evaluation of a sample of our data to assess the relative quality of our translation models further. We compare our results with Google Translate as the state-of-the-art translation tool.

The rest of the paper is structured as follow: Section 2 discusses the related work, which consists of parallel corpus collection and some En-Id MT approaches. Section 3 discusses the datasets that we use for training and testing. Section 4 describes the state-of-the-art and baseline MT methods that we use in our benchmark. Section 5 details our experiment settings and results, as well as discusses our findings and insights from the results. Finally, Section 6 concludes the paper and outlines some future work.

2. Related Work

The OPUS data portal (Tiedemann, 2012) provides a publicly available parallel dataset in 278 languages obtained from 55 open corpora,[1] although only 10 of them provide parallel data for English-Indonesian. Each corpus was collected from an open resource, and no manual data cleanup was carried out. Table 1 shows the statistics of the corpora containing English-Indonesian parallel sentences.

Corpus	doc's	sent's	en tok's	id tok's
OpenSubtitles v2018	9827	9.7M	72.8M	60.9M
Tanzil v1	45	0.5M	8.5M	15.4M
JW300 v1	8242	0.6M	10.0M	9.5M
Tatoeba v20190709	1	9.9K	11.0M	85.9K
QED v2.0a	2219	0.4M	4.8M	3.8M
GNOME v1	1347	0.5M	2.7M	2.3M
bible-uedin v1	2	62.2K	1.8M	1.4M
Ubuntu v14.10	398	96.5K	0.6M	0.3M
GlobalVoices v2017q3	562	14.5K	0.3M	0.3M
KDE4 v2	125	15.1K	86.0K	91.1K

Table 1: En-Id statistics shown on the OPUS webpage, November 2019

With over 9 million pairs, the OpenSubtitles dataset (Lison et al., 2018) represents around 80% of the En-Id sentence pairs in OPUS. The dataset is collected from the opensubtitles website.[2] Sentence pairs are extracted from two subtitles of different languages via time-slot alignment. Sometimes, there are time-slot mismatches because the subtitles are created using different sources of video with different play speeds and cut-off points. To combat the mismatches, two anchor points are selected as references to trim and to "stretch in/out" the other timestamps (Tiedemann, 2008). Although OPUS is an open platform to publish parallel data, some dataset is not integrated in OPUS yet. Wikimatrix (Schwenk et al., 2019) collects 135 millions parallel sentences from Wikipedia across 85 languages. Multilingual sentence alignment of Wikipedia pages is done by leveraging LASER (Artetxe and Schwenk, 2019b), a massively multilingual sentence embeddings of 93 languages trained on a subset of OPUS. Using LASER, each sentence pair x and y of two different languages is scored using a margin formula that is a ratio of their cosine similarity and the average cosine of their k nearest neighbors, as follows:

$$\text{margin}(x, y) = \frac{\cos(x, y)}{\displaystyle\sum_{z \in \text{NN}_k(x)} \frac{\cos(x, z)}{2k} + \sum_{z \in \text{NN}_k(y)} \frac{\cos(y, z)}{2k}}$$

A margin threshold is applied to decide whether x and y are mutual translations or not. It has been shown to be more consistent than the standard cosine similarity in determining correct translation pairs (Artetxe and Schwenk, 2019a).

---

[1] http://opus.nlpl.eu/ as of November 2019
[2] https://www.opensubtitles.org

Using this approach, Wikimatrix obtains at least 1 million En-Id sentences, depending on the threshold used.

Nevertheless, the data collected above has not yet been explored to build an English-Indonesian machine translation model. As English-Indonesian parallel data was considered to be low-resourced, attempts on data-driven machine translation are mostly a statistical-and-rule-based hybrid approach. Several examples include a general hybrid MT system where a rule-based morphological analysis is applied to generate an intermediate translation result which is then refined using an SMT model (Yulianti et al., 2011), a hybrid approach that analyzes Indonesian cliticization (Larasati, 2012a) and utterance disfluency (Shahih and Purwarianti, 2016) as a preprocessing step before feeding the training data into an SMT tool. Moving on from SMTs, Octoviani, et al. (2019) developed a neural-network-and-rule-based hybrid approach for phrase-based English-Indonesian Machine Translation. An RNN model is trained to classify the input phrase into a type. Then, a rule-based approach is applied for each phrase type to output the final translation. The approach was evaluated over a dataset of 70 pairs of phrases. Lastly, Hermanto et al.'s work (2015), which uses RNN, is the only work that we found within the topic of En-Id MT that utilizes NMT. They use the Pan Asia Networking Localization (PANL) dataset[3], which contains about 24,000 pairs of sentences, as their train and test data.

Due to the lack of distributed code from the previous work, we were not able to use them as our baselines. Instead, we use some variants of transformer-based models for our benchmark, which we will explain in details in Section 4.

3. Datasets

3.1. Existing Datasets

We collect data from OPUS (Tiedemann, 2012) which contains Open Subtitles (Lison et al., 2018) among other smaller datasets. Tanzil[4] and Bible-Uedin (Christodouloupoulos and Steedman, 2015) stores parallel Quran and Bible translations, respectively, while JW300 (Agić and Vulić, 2019) collects parallel sentences of Jehovah's Witness religious scripture and articles. Tatoeba[5] is a small database of sentences and translations in a general domain. GlobalVoices dataset[6] is a namesake of a multilingual news website,[7] from which its parallel sentences were crawled. Finally, GNOME[8], Ubuntu[9], and KDE4[10] datasets contain parallel software strings taken from their respective localization files.

We run the WikiMatrix (Schwenk et al., 2019) script to extract 1.8 million En-Id parallel sentences using a margin threshold value of 1.03 to obtain high-quality pairs in maximum number, as suggested in the paper. Other

---

[3] http://panl10n.net/english/OutputsIndonesia2.htm
[4] http://tanzil.net/trans/
[5] https://tatoeba.org/
[6] http://casmacat.eu/corpus/global-voices.html
[7] https://globalvoices.org/
[8] https://www.gnome.org/
[9] https://ubuntu.com/
[10] https://kde.org/

than OPUS and WikiMatrix, we find more, smaller datasets from the Web. The PANL dataset contains around 24,000 pairs of sentences manually aligned from news articles. IDENTIC (Larasati, 2012b) is a morphologically-enriched multidomain-dataset that combines the PANL dataset, a subset of Open Subtitles, and 164 manually-aligned sentences from BBC news articles. The Desmond86 dataset[11] contains parallel sentences obtained from BBC (news), Our Daily Bread (ODB)[12] (religion), SMERU[13] (research article), and AusAid[14] (humanitarian report). The Web Inventory of Transcribed and Translated Talks (WIT) (Cettolo et al., 2012)[15] released an extra dataset for the 2017 edition of International Workshop on Spoken Language Translation (IWSLT)[16], which also contains En-Id pairs extracted from TED talk videos. TALPCo contains high-quality pairs of short sentences originally translated from Japanese (Nomoto et al., 2018).

3.2. New Datasets

3.2.1. Bilingual BBC and BeritaJakarta

We use an earlier version of berita2bahasa.com crawler (Mitra, Sujiani and Negara, 2017) to crawl bilingual BBC[17] and bilingual BeritaJakarta[18] to extract parallel En-Id articles.[19] Each news article in the Bilingual BBC dataset is already paired and properly sentence-split. We observe that the translation style in this dataset is mostly one-to-one at the sentence level, meaning that most sentences are already paired. Although this results in less fluent translations in some cases, we have a straightforward sentence alignment with very few manual adjustments needed.

On the other hand, the Bilingual BeritaJakarta dataset is not yet aligned on the article-level. The Indonesian corpora contain 4000 timestamped articles, whereas the English contained 3000 articles. As the dataset was collected into a single clean text file, most of the article fingerprints are lost, and therefore using tools which rely on file fingerprints such as Bitextor (Esplá-Gomis and Forcada, 2009) is not feasible. We employ a timestamp-based alignment algorithm to find article pairs. First, for each language, articles published on the same date are grouped together. Then, two articles are paired following the order of publishing time, i.e., the first published article in Indonesian on a certain day is paired with the first published article in English on the same day, then the second article, then the third, etc. Mispairings are manually checked and fixed based on the titles. Then, we sentence-split the articles using NLTK (Loper and Bird, 2002). To ensure high-quality

pairs, sentence alignment is performed manually.

3.2.2. Ibn Majah Parallel Translation

Sunan Ibn Majah is a major hadith[20] collection and has been translated into several languages. We crawled http://carihadis.com/[21] for the Indonesian translation and https://www.islamicfinder.org/[22] for the English one. However, the Indonesian source uses an older version of Ibn Majah, and therefore uses different hadith indexes, which makes an automated alignment problematic. Therefore, we perform manual alignment instead.

3.2.3. Youtube Parallel Caption

We extract YouTube videos whose captions are available in both English and Indonesian from several channels e.g., TED, TEDx, Khan Academy, Kobasolo, Raditya Dika, and Londokampung. Channels selected are based on our manual observation, that is, whether they contain a good portion of videos having both English and Indonesian captions. The Indonesian captions are transcribed directly, whereas the English captions are translated by their fans. A YouTube caption comes in a series of chunks where each chunk contains the text, the start time, and the duration of that particular chunk. The captions are not well-aligned since the length of parallel sentences in Indonesian and English differ, and only a small part of them can fit into the screen. But, unlike Open Subtitles, all pairs of captions on YouTube follow the same video source; thus, no timestamp stretch or cut-off is necessary.

Alignment is done using a greedy algorithm. First, chunks without timestamp intersection in the other language are discarded. Then, starting from the first pair of chunks, we compute how much time they overlap with each other. For instance, if an Id chunk starts from 0:00 and ends at 0:03, while an En chunk starts from 0:01 and ends at 0:04, then altogether they span 4 seconds but they occur at the same time for only 2 seconds. We say that they are together $2/4 = 50\%$ of the time. We call this measure as the intersection of union (IoU) ratio. We say that a pair of chunks are aligned if their IoU ratio falls above a certain threshold. If a pair of chunks do not satisfy the threshold, then the next chunk is appended to the shorter one among the pair, until the threshold is reached. We experimented with various threshold values on a small, randomly selected and manually annotated data, and found that 0.8 is a good threshold for aligning the chunks.

3.3. Dataset Analysis

We analyze the collected datasets for their quality and their domain characteristics. We quantitatively explore the datasets, as shown in Table 2. We mainly assess their quality based on their sentence lengths, unique tokens, noise, and completeness of sentences. We find that most of them are good quality. However, we find some other to be lacking, and decide to drop them. That is, they are not included in our benchmark.

---

[11] https://github.com/desmond86/Indonesian-English-Bilingual-Corpus. Sentence alignment was manually done, which was confirmed by the dataset owner via private messages.

[12] https://odb.org/

[13] https://www.smeru.or.id/

[14] defunct and now replaced by the Australian Aid

[15] https://wit3.fbk.eu/

[16] http://workshop2017.iwslt.org/

[17] https://www.bbc.com/indonesia/topik/dwibahasa, 2013

[18] beritajakarta.id, 2013

[19] https://herrysujaini.blogspot.com/2013/04/kumpulan-mono-korpus-bahasa-indonesia.html

[20] A kind of Islamic religious scriptures

[21] No ToC prohibiting crawling

[22] Content download is allowed for non-commercial uses

Corpus	Abbr.	$|sent_{en-id}|$	$|tok_{en}|$	$|tok_{id}|$	$\overline{len_{en}}$	$\overline{len_{id}}$	$\overline{len_{ratio}}$	Domain/Content
OpenSubtitles v2018	OpenSub	9.3M	0.4M	0.5M	7.72	6.41	1.32	Movie
[*]Tanzil v1	Tanzil	0.4M	24.3K	25.4K	21.47	33.05	2.06	Religion
JW300 v1	JW300	0.6M	87.6K	83.2K	17.44	16.26	1.20	Religion
[*]Tatoeba v20190709	Tatoeba	9.9K	5.7K	6.9K	7.63	6.62	1.23	General
QED v2.0a	QED	0.3M	82.8K	85.9K	14.65	12.95	1.33	Talk, Lecture
[†]GNOME v1	GNOME	40.4K	29.9K	30.1K	22.19	19.70	1.22	Tech
bible-uedin v1	Bible	59.4K	17.2K	21.0K	29.49	24.03	1.43	Religion
[†]Ubuntu v14.10	Ubuntu	96.5K	37.9K	44.2K	6.26	6.18	1.25	Tech
GlobalVoices v2017q3	GV	14.4K	27.5K	27.3K	21.06	18.94	1.21	News
[†]KDE4 v2	KDE	14.8K	9.5K	10.9K	5.72	6.26	1.49	Tech
Wikimatrix (T=1.02)	Wiki[x]	1.8M	1M	0.9M	22.75	21.06	1.22	General
[∂]Desmond86	Dsm	40.4K	29.9K	30.1K	22.19	19.7	1.22	News, Religion, Science
[∂]IDENTIC v1	IDENTIC	27.3K	36K	35.4K	22.96	21.29	1.20	News, Movie
IWSLT 2017	IWSLT	0.1M	48.7K	48.2K	19.67	16.85	1.23	Conversation
PAN Localization	PANL	24K	35K	35.5K	22.96	21.29	1.20	News
TALPCo	TALPCo	1.4K	1.2K	1.2K	9.08	7.58	1.26	General
BBC-BeritaJakarta	BBC-BJ	3.9K	10.5K	10.1K	20.36	18.36	1.22	News
[†]**Ibn Majah**	IbnMj	0.8K	3.9K	4.6K	65.41	51.95	1.4	Religion
YouTube v0	YT	0.3M	60.4K	63.4K	9.3	7.93	1.28	Talk, Lecture, Movie

Table 2: Exploratory data analysis of all datasets. Abbr. denotes the abbreviation of the corpus names. $|X|$ denotes the unique count of a set X, whereas $\overline{Y}$ denotes the average of bag of values Y. len_{ratio} denotes the absolute ratio between the sentence length of the two languages, En and Id. The absolute ratio between two arbitrary numbers x, y is $\max(x/y, y/x)$. Bold items indicate new datasets. [†]datasets that are dropped, [∂]datasetes that are partially used, and [*]datasets with known problems but are used.

The Ubuntu and KDE4 datasets are taken from their respective software localization resources, and so we consider them to represent the tech domain. The majority of their "sentences" are short, incomplete, and noisy. For example:

- En: "%s: access ACL '%s': %s at entry %d"

- Id: "%s: akses ACL '%s': %s at masukan %d"

Therefore, the data as it is right now would not be very useful, and further refinement and filtering are necessary. The GNOME dataset, the third representative of the tech domain, unlike the other two, has higher-quality pairs. However, we could not find any other dataset within the same domain, so we decide to drop the tech domain altogether.[23] The Ibn Majah dataset contains sentences that are too long and need to be split, which is difficult due to inconsistent usage of splitting punctuations (commas, periods, colons, and semicolons) in the corpus. We decide to drop this dataset in our benchmark. The Desmond dataset contains a few numbers of pairs in the domain of Science, which are dropped. Lastly, the IDENTIC dataset has some intersection with the PANL and Open Subtitle datasets. Therefore we only consider the non-intersecting sentences.

After filtering out low-quality and redundant data, we combine the datasets falling under the same domain. News domain consists of news articles. Religious domain consists of religious manuscripts or articles. These articles are different from news as they are not in a formal, informative style. Instead, they are written to advocate and inspire religious values, often times citing biblical or quranic anecdotes. Next, we combine all datasets that come from human speech (movie, talk, and lecture) into the conversation domain. Lastly, we merge datasets that cover broad topics into the general domain. Then, for each domain, we split it into a train, validation, and test data. The result is shown in Table 3.

Domain	Corpus	Sent's	Split	$nsim_{V,T}$
News	PANL	24k	train	3.3
	GV	14.4K	train	
	BBC-BJ	3.9K	valid+test	
Religion	Tanzil	0.4M	train	5.3
	JW300	0.6M	train	
	Bible	59.4K	train	
	Dsm$_{ODB}$	9k	valid+test	
Conversation	OpenSub	9.3M	all	18.5
	QED	0.4M	all	
	IWSLT	0.1M	all	
	YT	0.3M	all	
General	Wiki[x]	1.8M	all	7.3
	Tatoeba	9.9K	train	
	TALPCo	1.4K	all	

Table 3: Data split and n-gram similarity between validation and training data for each domain.

For news and religion domain, we choose an exclusive corpus:

- BBC-BJ for news, and
- Desmond ODB (Our Daily Bread, the religion part of Desmond dataset) for religion,

to be our validation and test data because (1) they are manually curated and of high-quality, (2) they are much smaller

---

[23]Experimentally, this is to avoid overfitting our model if it is trained on the tech domain with only one dataset.

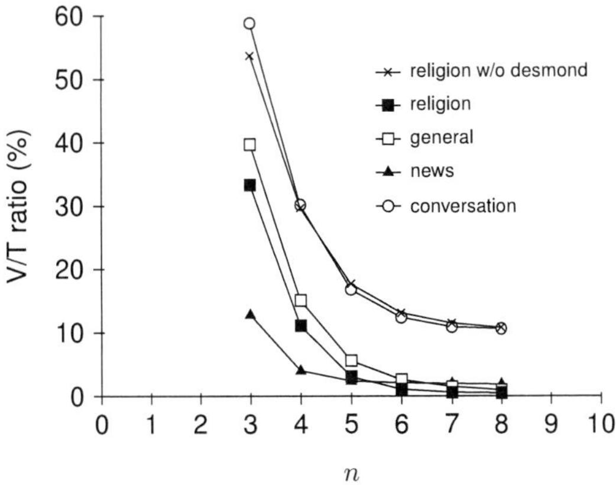

Figure 1: n-gram occurrences ratio between validation and test set across domains for n from 3 to 8.

than the rest of training data and therefore do not sacrifice too much portion of data that could have been for training instead, and (3) they have similar sentence length compared to the training data. There is no such corpus for the conversation domain and the general domain. The datasets in the conversation domain are all automatically aligned and therefore are noisy. For the general domain, both Tatoeba and TALPCo are manually curated, but their sentences (especially Tatoeba) are very short compared to Wikimatrix. Therefore, for these two datasets, we do a random split involving all datasets in the domain for validation and testing, each having 2000 unique pairs not present in the training set. For the general domain, we mix shorter sentences from TALPCo and the longer ones from Wikimatrix as our validation and test data. We observe that Tatoeba has similar types of high-quality sentences like TALPCo has, albeit shorter. Therefore we choose TALPCo to be in the validation and test sets instead, because longer sentences mean more difficult and meaningful evaluation.

To see the difference between these two split settings, we compute the rate of phrases (in terms of n-grams) that appear in validation set sentences that also appear in the training set sentences. Figure 1 shows this computation for $3 \leq n \leq 8$ for each domain. It shows that domains without an exclusive corpus for the validation set has a higher n-gram intersections between the validation set and the training set, which means that a model trained on the domain might be overfitted for the dataset and it might prove difficult to see how such a model generalizes to unseen dataset within the same domain. To further emphasize this point, we tried to built another split for the religion domain without the Desmond dataset, that is, the split involves all the other three datasets: Tanzil, Bible, and JW300. The result is that the validation and test sets share significantly more n-grams.

We further compute a weighted average of the occurrence ratios across ns, that is

$$\text{nsim}(V, T) = \frac{\sum_{n=3}^{8} n \times 100 \frac{\text{c}(n-\text{gram in } V \text{ appearing in } T)}{\text{c}(n-\text{gram in } V)}}{\sum_{n=a}^{b} n}$$

where c is a counting function, V is the validation set, and T is the training set. The results of the weighted average of each domain is shown in Table 3, where the conversation domain is shown to have the highest $\text{nsim}(V, T)$ of 18.5. In the next subsections, we discuss some special characteristics of each domain.

3.3.1. News

Some sentence pairs in the news domain suffer from the inter-sentence context-preservation issue. For instance, we sometimes find that a single sentence is aligned to two (usually shorter) sentences in the other language in order to capture the whole context of the single sentence. Another observation is the usage of pronouns, which loses context whenever the article is split into sentences and then paired. For example:

- En: **The firm** says the posts will go around ...

- Id: **Sony** mengatakan PHK karyawan dilakukan ...

In this example, "Sony" as an entity is described as "The firm". Readers should understand the connection if presented with the whole article, but not as independent sentences.

Some sentences are appended with extra information to help the readers understand the news better based on their local knowledge. One of the most common examples is a converted currency, as shown in the example below.

- "Kalau jauh misalnya di Indramayu, bisa 2,5 juta - 3 juta Rupiah."

- "If it is far, in Indramayu for instance, it could be around 2,5 - 3 million Rupiah (**\$250 - \$300**)."

Specifically, in Global Voices, we find translated tweets or Instagram posts, as this news site often include people's reaction on social media in their articles. This part of the text is out-of-domain within the context of news. Furthermore, we find inconsistency in translating or copying the tweet's usernames or tags.

3.3.2. Religion

The Tanzil dataset is a Quran translation dataset which has a relatively-imbalanced sentence length between the two languages, evidenced in Table 2, where an average Indonesian sentence in this dataset is about 50% longer than an average English one. Furthermore, an average pair of sentences in this dataset would, on average, have one of them twice as long as the other. However, we still decide to include the dataset in the domain to avoid overfitting because the remaining datasets are all about Christianity.

Another interesting property in the religion domain corpus is the localized names, for example, David to Daud, Mary to Maryam, Gabriel to Jibril, and more. In contrast, entity names are usually kept unchanged in other domains.

We also find quite a handful of Indonesian translations of JW300 are missing the end sentence dot (.), even though the end sentence dot is present in their English counterpart. Lastly, we also find some inconsistency in the transliteration, for example praying is sometimes written as "salat" or "shalat", or repentance as "tobat" or "taubat".

3.3.3. General

The Tatoeba dataset contains short sentences. However, they contain high-quality full-sentence pairs with precise translation and is widely used in previous work in other languages (Artetxe and Schwenk, 2019b). Due to its simplicity, we do not use Tatoeba as our test and validation sets. We find that the Wikipedia scraper for Wikimatrix is faulty in some cases, causing some noise coming from unfiltered markup tags.

3.3.4. Conversation

Our conversational domain corpus is translated from English. Hence the Indonesian sentences are written in formal language. In practice, Indonesian used informal language in speech, most of the time. In addition, we also used informal language in a conversational situation such as in social media or text messages.

4. Methods

4.1. Transformer-based Machine Translation

Transformer based model (Vaswani et al., 2017) is the current state-of-the-art for neural machine translation (Bojar et al., 2018). Therefore we adopt the standard Transformer-base encoder-decoder model as one of our baseline models.

4.2. Language-Model Pretraining

Generative pretraining has been proved to be effective in improving sentence encoders on downstream tasks. We use two language modeling objectives, Masked Language Modeling (MLM) to leverage our vastly available monolingual corpora and Translation Language Modeling (TLM) to make the network learns alignment between languages better. (Devlin et al., 2018; Radford et al., 2018; Lample and Conneau, 2019)

Although both MLM and TLM objectives can be extended to multiple languages, we only pretrain the base Transformer using Indonesian and English dataset since the network itself will only be used on tasks involving Indonesian and English languages. For the MLM objective, the Indonesian monolingual dataset was collected from Leipzig corpora (Goldhahn et al., 2012), and the English monolingual dataset was collected from WMT'07 and WMT'08.[24] Both datasets come from the news domain and are truncated at 4.8M sentences because of GPU resource limitation. For the TLM objective, Tatoeba and PANL datasets are used.

4.3. Google Translate

Google Translate is arguably one of the best public translation services available. However, benchmarking with Google Translate is tricky: Their model is regularly updated. Hence the result is not reproducible. We also cannot guarantee that our validation or test set is not present in their training data. However, we still argue that comparing our results with theirs is beneficial.

5. Experiments and Result

5.1. Setup

We run our Transformer experiment with XLM Toolkit on a single GPU. We use the Transformer base architecture,

consisting of 6 encoder and decoder layers with 8 attention heads. The feed-forward unit-size is 2048, and the embedding size is 512. We increase the batch size from the default 32 to 160 to reduce the gradient noise (Wang et al., 2013; Smith et al., 2017), which shown to improve the model's quality (Ott et al., 2018; Popel and Bojar, 2018; Aji and Heafield, 2019). We use Adam optimizer (Kingma and Ba, 2014) with a learning rate of 0.0001, $\beta_1 = 0.9, \beta_2 = 0.999$. We train our language model with the same Toolkit. Performance is measured with a BLEU score (Papineni et al., 2002) by using sacreBLEU script (Post, 2018).

5.2. Model Evaluation

We first benchmark the significance of language-model pretraining for the Transformer. For this purpose, we train both vanilla Transformer and Transformer with language model pretraining for our news and general domain dataset. From the result shown in Table 4, we can see that the Transformer with language model pretraining outperforms its vanilla counterpart. We can also see that model trained in general domain outperforms model trained in news domain, therefore suggesting that a standard model with more data is better than a low-resource training with language model pretraining. For the next experiments, we will use a Transformer with a pretrained language model.

5.3. Cross Domain Evaluation

We explore the performance when trained across different domains. Our results shown in Table 5 suggest that the model is overfitted towards its specific domain. Model trained with the news domain dataset performed worst due to lack of resource. By combining every dataset, we can see the best performance across every domain. This result is comparable with Google Translate. We picked our best model, which is trained in all training set and evaluate the BLEU on test sets, which can be seen in Table 6.

5.4. Human Evaluation

We do not have an annotated parallel corpus for English-Indonesian. Our corpus, including the valid and test set, are generated from the crawled data. We discussed previously in section 3. that the currently available dataset are not fully parallel. Therefore, measuring the quality with BLEU only might not be representative.

For human evaluation, we select random sentences from each domain. We present three translations: Reference, Google Translate, and our output in random order to our human evaluators. We measure the quality in 2 scores:

- Fluency (1-5): How fluent the translation is, regardless of the correctness.

- Adequacy (1-5): How correct is the translation, given the source.

To ensure reliability of the scores, each and all sentences are assigned to 3 scorers. The final score is the averaged score across three evaluators, as shown in Table 7. Because we have more than two annotators and the scores are ordinal, we use Spearman's ρ to obtain a moderately-high average agreement between annotators of 0.53 for fluency and 0.56 for adequacy out of 240 sentences.

---

[24]http://www.casmacat.eu/corpus/news-commentary.html

Training Data	EN to ID evaluation (valid set)					ID to EN evaluation (valid set)				
	News	Religious	Conv	General	Average	News	Religious	Conv	General	Average
Transformer										
News	10.2	6.5	9.8	8.2	8.7	9.6	6.3	12.3	8.9	9.3
General	18.8	15.2	15.8	26.8	19.1	13.1	10.2	9.8	25.3	15.4
Transformer + Language Pretraining										
News	17.4	11.5	14.8	14.8	14.6	15.1	10.6	19.6	16.3	15.4
General	20.0	15.6	15.3	27.8	19.7	16.6	13.7	13.3	28.8	18.1

Table 4: Performance of different baselines across News (low-resource) and General (high-resource) domain.

Training Data	EN to ID evaluation (valid set)					ID to EN evaluation (valid set)				
	News	Religious	Conv	General	Average	News	Religious	Conv	General	Average
News	**17.4**	11.5	14.8	14.8	14.6	15.1	10.6	**19.6**	16.3	15.4
Religious	16.5	**21.5**	15.4	18.9	18.1	15.1	**20.2**	5.6	19.3	15.1
Conv	18.9	15.2	**28.0**	21.0	20.8	15.5	16.6	**33.1**	18.8	21.0
General	20.0	15.6	15.3	**27.8**	19.7	16.6	13.7	13.3	**28.8**	18.1

(a) Model generally performs well when evaluated with in-domain set. It performs poorly otherwise. An exception can be seen in the low-resource news domain.

Training Data	EN to ID evaluation (valid set)					ID to EN evaluation (valid set)				
	News	Religious	Conv	General	Average	News	Religious	Conv	General	Average
Transformer + Language Pretraining										
News + general	21.9	17.2	15.3	27.0	20.4	18.4	15.4	14.6	28.8	19.3
Relig.+ general	24.0	21.3	16.9	27.9	22.5	19.9	22.3	16.1	28.5	21.7
Conv + general	21.8	18.2	27.7	27.5	23.8	18.2	18.0	33.6	27.9	24.4
All	**24.6**	**21.6**	**27.8**	**28.1**	**25.5**	**20.5**	**22.5**	**33.3**	**27.9**	**26.1**
Google Translate										
-	25.0	23.8	27.0	26.3	25.5	25.0	29.1	28.9	28.8	28.0

(b) Adding general-domain to the training set improves the performance across different domains. Ultimately, combining all dataset yields the best results.

Table 5: Cross-domain evaluation of Transformer with language pretraining

Test Domain	EN to ID	ID to EN
News	24.4	20.2
Religious	21.3	22.1
Conversation	27.3	32.4
General	28.1	28.9
Average	25.3	25.9

Table 6: Evaluation on test set. We compare our model trained with all dataset with Google Translate (GT).

	News	Relig.	Conv	General	Avg
Fluency					
Corpus	4.78	4.73	4.63	4.63	4.69
Ours	4.44	4.22	4.62	4.21	4.37
Google	4.26	3.85	4.53	3.59	4.06
Adequecy					
Corpus	4.34	4.58	3.92	3.92	4.19
Ours	4.05	4.09	4.38	4.1	4.15
Google	4.27	3.99	4.6	3.92	4.2

Table 7: Human evaluation score across different domains.

The reference translation is the most fluent across every domain. This result is expected, as the reference is written by humans. Reference translation's adequacy scored equally on average, compared to the rest. Our reference is crawled; therefore, it contains several issues, as mentioned in section 3.3.. One main problem in reference translation is that they are translated with document level in mind, therefore reducing adequacy as encapsulated sentence-based translation. This is especially true in conversational, where the reference was translated from the whole session (i.e., talk, or vlog). One example can be seen below:

Source	”- Nope, they're shutting us down.”
Ref	”- Tidak, misi ditunda.”
Ours	”- Tidak, mereka menutup kita”.
Google Translate	”- Tidak, mereka menutup kita.”

The reference is literally translated as ”- No, mission postponed.”, which is not the correct translation of the source. However, the reference is in fact acceptable when given the whole document.

6. Conclusions and Future Work

We showed that Bahasa Indonesia has improved from the preconception of being a low-resource language in the context of English MT. We have collected scattered English-Indonesian parallel data and introduced some new parallel datasets through automatic and manual alignments. Our collected datasets numbers in more than 10 million pairs of sentences. We evaluated and categorized those datasets into several domains: news, religion, general, and conversation. We created a standardized split for evaluation to open a pathway for objective evaluation for future En-Id MT research. Our Transformer-based baseline trained with multidomain dataset produces a comparable quality compared to Google Translate and is robust against domain changes. However, we acknowledge that some improvements to our datasetes are necessary. Some important domains like news are still behind in terms of training data, and evidently, its BLEU score is still lacking compared to the general and conversational domain. Furthermore, our manual evaluation has shown that some of our datasets contain noise, especially in the conversation and general domain where the noisy data is still used in validation and testing. In the future, manual data filtering or cleansing on these datasets is important to ensure that we have a standard benchmark that is clean and unbiased.

7. Bibliographical References

Agić, Ž. and Vulić, I. (2019). Jw300: A wide-coverage parallel corpus for low-resource languages. In *Proceedings of the 57th Annual Meeting of the Association for Computational Linguistics*, pages 3204–3210.

Aji, A. F. and Heafield, K. (2019). Making asynchronous stochastic gradient descent work for transformers. In *Proceedings of the 3rd Workshop on Neural Generation and Translation*, pages 80–89, Hong Kong, November. Association for Computational Linguistics.

Artetxe, M. and Schwenk, H. (2019a). Margin-based parallel corpus mining with multilingual sentence embeddings. In *Proceedings of the 57th Annual Meeting of the Association for Computational Linguistics*, pages 3197–3203, Florence, Italy, July. Association for Computational Linguistics.

Artetxe, M. and Schwenk, H. (2019b). Massively multilingual sentence embeddings for zero-shot cross-lingual transfer and beyond. *Transactions of the Association for Computational Linguistics*, 7:597–610.

Bojar, O., Federmann, C., Fishel, M., Graham, Y., Haddow, B., Huck, M., Koehn, P., and Monz, C. (2018). Findings of the 2018 conference on machine translation (wmt18). In *Proceedings of the Third Conference on Machine Translation (WMT), Volume 2: Shared Task Papers*, pages 272–307. Association for Computational Linguistics, 10.

Cettolo, M., Girardi, C., and Federico, M. (2012). Wit3: Web inventory of transcribed and translated talks. In *Conference of European Association for Machine Translation*, pages 261–268.

Christodouloupoulos, C. and Steedman, M. (2015). A massively parallel corpus: the bible in 100 languages. *Language resources and evaluation*, 49(2):375–395.

Devlin, J., Chang, M.-W., Lee, K., and Toutanova, K. (2018). Bert: Pre-training of deep bidirectional transformers for language understanding. *arXiv preprint arXiv:1810.04805*.

Eberhard, D. M., Simons, G. F., and Fennig, C. D. (2019). *Ethnologue: Languages of the World*. SIL International, Dallas, Texas, 22nd edition.

Esplá-Gomis, M. and Forcada, M. L. (2009). Bitextor, a free/open-source software to harvest translation memories from multilingual websites. *Proceedings of MT Summit XII, Ottawa, Canada. Association for Machine Translation in the Americas*.

Goldhahn, D., Eckart, T., and Quasthoff, U. (2012). Building large monolingual dictionaries at the leipzig corpora collection: From 100 to 200 languages. In *LREC*, volume 29, pages 31–43.

Hermanto, A., Adji, T. B., and Setiawan, N. A. (2015). Recurrent neural network language model for english-indonesian machine translation: Experimental study. In *2015 International Conference on Science in Information Technology (ICSITech)*, pages 132–136. IEEE.

Kingma, D. P. and Ba, J. (2014). Adam: A method for stochastic optimization. *arXiv preprint arXiv:1412.6980*.

Lample, G. and Conneau, A. (2019). Cross-lingual language model pretraining. *arXiv preprint arXiv:1901.07291*.

Larasati, S. D. (2012a). Handling indonesian clitics: A dataset comparison for an indonesian-english statistical machine translation system. In *Proceedings of the 26th Pacific Asia Conference on Language, Information, and Computation*, pages 146–152.

Larasati, S. D. (2012b). Identic corpus: Morphologically enriched indonesian-english parallel corpus. In *LREC*, pages 902–906.

Lison, P., Tiedemann, J., and Kouylekov, M. (2018). Opensubtitles2018: Statistical rescoring of sentence alignments in large, noisy parallel corpora. In *Proceedings of the Eleventh International Conference on Language Resources and Evaluation (LREC 2018)*.

Loper, E. and Bird, S. (2002). Nltk: the natural language toolkit. *arXiv preprint cs/0205028*.

Mitra, V., Sujaini, H., and Negara, A. B. P. (2017). Rancang bangun aplikasi web scraping untuk korpus paralel indonesia-inggris dengan metode html dom. *Jurnal Sistem dan Teknologi Informasi (JUSTIN)*, 5(1):36–41.

Nomoto, H., Okano, K., Moeljadi, D., and Sawada, H. (2018). Tufs asian language parallel corpus (talpco). In *Proceedings of the Twenty-Fourth Annual Meeting of the Association for Natural Language Processing*, pages 436–439.

Octoviani, W., Fachrurrozi, M., Yusliani, N., Febriady, M., and Firdaus, A. (2019). English–indonesian phrase translation using recurrent neural network and adj technique. In *Journal of Physics: Conference Series*, volume 1196, page 012007. IOP Publishing.

Ott, M., Edunov, S., Grangier, D., and Auli, M. (2018). Scaling neural machine translation. In *Proceedings of the Third Conference on Machine Translation: Research Papers*, pages 1–9.

Papineni, K., Roukos, S., Ward, T., and Zhu, W.-J. (2002). Bleu: a method for automatic evaluation of machine translation. In *Proceedings of the 40th annual meeting on association for computational linguistics*, pages 311–318. Association for Computational Linguistics.

Popel, M. and Bojar, O. (2018). Training tips for the transformer model. *The Prague Bulletin of Mathematical Linguistics*, 110(1):43–70.

Post, M. (2018). A call for clarity in reporting BLEU scores. In *Proceedings of the Third Conference on Machine Translation: Research Papers*, pages 186–191,

Belgium, Brussels, October. Association for Computational Linguistics.

Radford, A., Narasimhan, K., Salimans, T., and Sutskever, I. (2018). Improving language understanding by generative pre-training. *URL https://s3-us-west-2. amazonaws. com/openai-assets/researchcovers/languageunsupervised/language understanding paper. pdf.*

Riza, H. (2008). Resources report on languages of indonesia. In *Proceedings of the 6th Workshop on Asian Language Resources.*

Schwenk, H., Chaudhary, V., Sun, S., Gong, H., and Guzmán, F. (2019). Wikimatrix: Mining 135m parallel sentences in 1620 language pairs from wikipedia. *arXiv preprint arXiv:1907.05791.*

Shahih, K. M. and Purwarianti, A. (2016). Utterance disfluency handling in indonesian-english machine translation. In *2016 International Conference On Advanced Informatics: Concepts, Theory And Application (ICAICTA)*, pages 1–5. IEEE.

Smith, S. L., Kindermans, P.-J., Ying, C., and Le, Q. V. (2017). Don't decay the learning rate, increase the batch size. *arXiv preprint arXiv:1711.00489.*

Tiedemann, J. (2008). Synchronizing translated movie subtitles. In *LREC.*

Tiedemann, J. (2012). Parallel data, tools and interfaces in opus. In *Lrec*, volume 2012, pages 2214–2218.

Vaswani, A., Shazeer, N., Parmar, N., Uszkoreit, J., Jones, L., Gomez, A. N., Kaiser, Ł., and Polosukhin, I. (2017). Attention is all you need. In *Advances in Neural Information Processing Systems*, pages 5998–6008.

Wang, C., Chen, X., Smola, A. J., and Xing, E. P. (2013). Variance reduction for stochastic gradient optimization. In *Advances in Neural Information Processing Systems*, pages 181–189.

Yulianti, E., Budi, I., Hidayanto, A. N., Manurung, H. M., and Adriani, M. (2011). Developing indonesian-english hybrid machine translation system. In *2011 International Conference on Advanced Computer Science and Information Systems*, pages 265–270. IEEE.

Proceedings of the 13th Workshop on Building and Using Comparable Corpora, pages 44–48
Language Resources and Evaluation Conference (LREC 2020), Marseille, 11–16 May 2020
© European Language Resources Association (ELRA), licensed under CC-BY-NC

Reducing the Search Space for Parallel Sentences in Comparable Corpora

Rémi Cardon, Natalia Grabar
CNRS, Univ. Lille, UMR 8163 STL - Savoirs Textes Langage
F-59000 Lille, France
{remi.cardon, natalia.grabar}@univ-lille.fr

Abstract

This paper describes and evaluates three methods for reducing the research space for parallel sentences in monolingual comparable corpora. Basically, when searching for parallel sentences between two comparable documents, all the possible sentence pairs between the documents have to be considered, which introduces a great degree of imbalance between parallel pairs and non-parallel pairs. This is a problem because, even with a highly performing algorithm, a lot of noise will be present in the extracted results, thus introducing a need for an extensive and costly manual check phase. We propose to study how we can drastically reduce the number of sentence pairs that have to be fed to a classifier so that the results can be manually handled. We work on a manually annotated subset obtained from a French comparable corpus.

Keywords: Parallel corpus creation, syntax, French

1. Introduction

Monolingual parallel corpora are useful for a variety of sequence-to-sequence tasks in natural language processing, such as text simplification (Xu et al., 2015), paraphrase acquisition (Deléger and Zweigenbaum, 2009) or style transfer (Jhamtani et al., 2017).

In order to build such parallel corpora, the typical approach is to start from comparable corpora and extract sentence pairs that share the same meaning. For instance, the participants of the BUCC 2017 shared task had to address this problem using bilingual corpora (Zweigenbaum et al., 2017). One major obstacle is that, when considering two documents A and B, every single sentence from A has to be evaluated against every single sentence of B, when document metadata cannot be used to make assumptions as to where to look for corresponding sentences. This produces a large amount of noise, and even with highly performing algorithms, the result of the extraction has to be manually checked for quality. With large volumes of data, this can be extremely costly. This is a known issue when working with comparable corpora (Zhang and Zweigenbaum, 2017). Yet, the issue is either not mentioned in works on parallel corpora creation from comparable corpora, or external information is used, such as metadata (Smith et al., 2010), which helps a lot the task.

In our work, we propose and evaluate methods for filtering out sentences and sentence pairs that have no chance of being of interest for the building of a parallel corpus. Hence, the purpose is to reduce the amount of manual check that needs to be performed on the output of a classifier.

2. Data collection and pre-processing

To perform our experiments, we work with a French comparable corpus containing biomedical documents with technical and simplified contents (Grabar and Cardon, 2018). The corpus is composed of three subcorpora: drug information for medical practitioners and patients released by the French Ministry of Health[1], medical literature reviews and

their manual simplification released by the Cochrane foundation[2], and encyclopedia articles from Wikipedia[3] and Vikidia[4]. The documents are organised in pairs where the texts address the same topic for different audiences, so that the delivered information and the phrasing are not identical. More importantly, the order in which the information is delivered is not the same, which means that the document structure cannot be used for assuming where to look for parallel sentences.

For our experiments, we took 39 randomly selected document pairs from that corpus and manually annotated them for two types of sentence pairs :

- Equivalence : the sentences mean the same, but they are not identical;

- Inclusion : the meaning of one sentence is included in the other one, where additional information can also be found. This retains information about sentence splitting or merging and about information deletion or addition.

The documents are pre-processed for syntactic POS-tagging and syntactic analysis into constituents (Kitaev and Klein, 2018). In the manually annotated set, only sentences that have a verb are kept. This yields 266 sentence pairs: 136 equivalent pairs, and 130 inclusion pairs (56 in one direction, 74 in the other one).

For the automatic processing, we produced the whole possible combinations of sentences within each of the 39 document pairs, and ended up with 1,164,407 sentence pairs. Thus, given that, out of more than one million possible pairs, only 266 sentence pairs are considered as useful for the parallel corpus creation, we observe a high degree of imbalance: little less than 4,400:1. Our purpose is to reduce this imbalance for facilitating the search of parallel sentences and improving the overall quality of the results.

---

[1] http://base-donnees-publique.
medicaments.gouv.fr/

[2] https://france.cochrane.org/
revues-cochrane

[3] https://fr.wikipedia.org/

[4] https://fr.vikidia.org/

3. Method

In order to address that extremely high degree of imbalance, we propose to investigate three methods using formal and syntactic indicators:

- First method is based on the number of tokens in sentences. Hence, each candidate sentence must contain at least five tokens. This permits to consider sentences that are grammatically complete and convey some semantics. We set that value to five because that is the length of the shortest sentence in the set with the manual annotations;

- Second method prevents from producing pairs with identical sentences;

- Third method relies on syntactic information. We base our work on a method that uses constituency parsing for measuring similarity between sentences in a monolingual setting (Duran et al., 2014). In the original work, the authors detect similar words in sentences and assign a similarity score that is computed by looking at similar labels of nodes that contain similar words. The process is described in Figure 1. It is difficult to adapt that method as it is described in the paper. The main reason is that it relies heavily on a table that establishes which grammatical categories for constituents are similar to one another. It is made for English and there is no indication as to how it was built. Nonetheless, we make the assumption that adopting a similar approach could help in the process of weeding out undesired pairs for building a parallel corpus. Hence, instead of calculating a similarity score, we just choose between keeping the sentence pair as a candidate for a classifier, or rejecting it. For a given pair, we produce a syntactic tree for each of the two sentences. Then, if both sentences contain a verb, we compare all the leaves (i.e. words) of the trees, except the ones that are part of the stop words list. The list contains 83 items that are grammatical words, such as determiners or prepositions for example. If we find two identical words, we look at their parents nodes' labels. If those are identical, we keep the sentence in the candidates list. That process is illustrated in Algorithm 1 below. We also perform the same approach but instead of stopping if the parents nodes' labels are not identical, we go up a level to perform the same comparison, and up another level if the previous comparison was not successful. As soon as one comparison succeeds, we keep the sentence pair in the candidates list. This other approach is illustrated in Algorithm 2. That movement to the third parent of the leaves is what is chosen in the method which inspires this work, we chose to implement it to learn how the depth of exploration influences our filtering.

To parse the sentences in order to obtain their syntactic tree with constituents, we use the Berkeley Neural Parser and the language model that is provided with it for French, with the `benepar` Python library (Kitaev and Klein, 2018). The, we use the NLTK's `Tree` library (Bird et al., 2009) for tree manipulation and exploration.

Data: A pair of syntactic trees (T_1 and T_2), a list of stop words (SW)

Result: Boolean

Boolean ← False;

if *one verb is found in both sentences* **then**

  foreach *leaf in T_1 (L_1) not found in SW* **do**

    foreach *leaf in T_2 (L_2) not found in SW* **do**

      if *L_1 is identical to L_2* **then**

        if *L_1's parent node's label is identical to L_2's parent node's label* **then**

          | Boolean ← True;

        else

          | nothing;

        end

      else

        | nothing;

      end

    end

  end

else

  | nothing;

end

return Boolean;

Algorithm 1: Filtering method only looking at the immediate parent nodes of the leaves

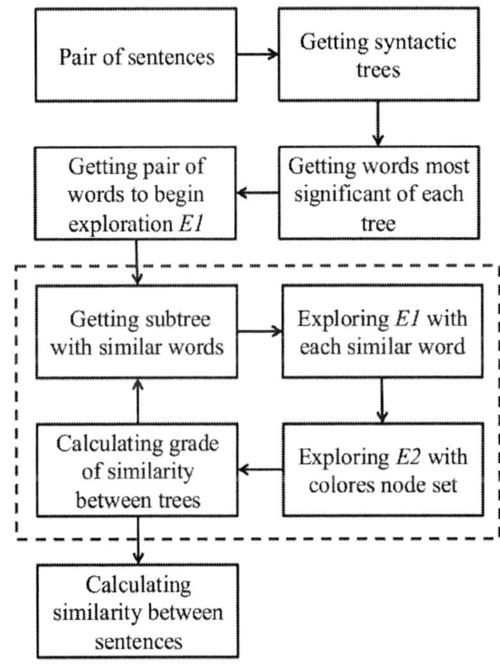

Figure 1: The similarity method described in (Duran et al., 2014)

4. Evaluation

We evaluate the results obtained in three different ways:

- we compare the number of initial sentence pairs to the number of remaining sentence pairs after the filtering,

- we check whether the removed pairs are manually an-

Remaining Pairs	*Unfiltered*	*FI*	*Syntax Depth 1*	*Syntax Depth 3*
Total	1,164,407	409,530	16,879	21,428
Equivalent	136	136	94	94
Inclusion	130	130	94	100

Table 1: Pairs remaining after the various filtering methods.

Data: A pair of syntactic trees (T_1 and T_2), a list of stop words (*SW*)
Result: Boolean
Boolean $\leftarrow$ False;
if *one verb is found in both sentences* **then**
  foreach *leaf in T_1 (L_1) not found in SW* **do**
    foreach *leaf in T_2 (L_2) not found in SW* **do**
      if L_1 *is identical to* L_2 **then**
        if L_1*'s parent node's label (P_1) is identical to* L_2*'s parent node's label (P_2)* **then**
         | Boolean $\leftarrow$ True;
        else
         if P_1*'s parent node's label (PP_1) is identical to* P_2*'s parent node's label (PP_2)* **then**
          | Boolean $\leftarrow$ True;
         else
          if PP_1*'s parent node's label is identical to* PP_2*'s parent node's label* **then**
           | Boolean $\leftarrow$ True;
          else
           | nothing;
          end
         end
        end
      else
        | nothing;
      end
    end
  end
else
  | nothing;
end
return Boolean;
Algorithm 2: Filtering method looking up to the third parent node of the leaves

notated as parallel, be it equivalence or inclusion relation, in the reference dataset,

- we give the remaining data to a random forest classifier algorithm, such as done in a previous work (Cardon and Grabar, 2019), and evaluate recall and precision of the output.

The overall goal is to remove as many negative examples as possible, while preserving the positive examples.

5. Results and Discussion

We first look at how the volume of data is reduced further to the filtering operations. The first column in Table 1 shows the number of raw sentence pairs, the second colum indicates the number of pairs after using the formal indicators (FI), the third and fourth columns show the number of pairs remaining when using the syntactic filter, respectively with looking at the first syntactic parent node and up to the third parent node. The formal indicators are applied before the syntactic filters. The syntactic filters are used independently from one another.

We can see that the simple formal indicators reduce the total number of sentence pairs by 65% (from 1,164,407 to 409,530 sentence pairs). These two indicators were defined on the basis of observation of our data. They are very straightforward and we expected that no positive example (equivalent and inclusion pairs) would be lost in the process. This hypothesis is verified indeed: all the good candidates for parallel pairs are kept at this step.

Starting from the 409,530 pairs obtained after this first filter, we can see that both syntactic filters lead to a huge reduction of the volume of remaining sentence pairs:

- when using depth 1 leaves 16,879 pairs ($\sim$96% reduction) remain,

- when using depth 3 leaves 21,428 pairs ($\sim$95% reduction) remain.

The downside is that a substantial amount of positive examples is also lost in the process:

- 42 out of 136 ($\sim$30%) for equivalent pairs with both depths used,

- 36 out of 130 ($\sim$27%) for inclusion pairs with depth 1, 32 out of 130 ($\sim$24%) for inclusion pairs with depth 3.

The over 95% reduction with the syntax filter on data that were already greatly reduced complies with our initial goal. Yet, we lose several good candidates for parallel sentences. Hence, we look at the positive examples that were rejected by the syntactic filter in order to understand why it is the case and how we can address this issue.

For instance, consider the following sentence pair:

- *Dans le cas où le patient devrait arrêter le traitement, il est recommandé de réduire progressivement la posologie. (In case the patient should stop the treatment, it is recommended to decrease the dose progressively.)*

- *L'arrêt du traitement doit se faire de manière progressive. (The cessation of treatment must be done progressively.)*

Set	Unfiltered			FI			Syntax Depth 1			Syntax Depth 3		
	P	R	F1	P	R	F1	P	R	F1	P	R	F1
Equivalent Neg.	1.00	1.00	1.00	1.00	1.00	1.00	1.00	1.00	1.00	1.00	1.00	1.00
Equivalent Pos.	0.79	0.43	0.55	0.82	0.32	0.46	0.75	0.39	0.51	0.84	0.40	0.54
Inclusion Neg.	1.00	1.00	1.00	1.00	1.00	1.00	1.00	1.00	1.00	1.00	1.00	1.00
Inclusion Pos.	0.71	0.09	0.17	0.50	0.16	0.24	0.71	0.15	0.24	0.56	0.15	0.24

Table 2: Precision, Recall and F1 scores on the different sets of sentence pairs with classification.

The reason why this kind of sentence pairs is rejected is because the labels of parent nodes for identical words (such as *traitement (treatment)* in this example) differ in the trees produced by the syntactic parser. Indeed, in the first sentence, *le traitement (the treatment)* is labelled as an NP-OBJ, while it is labelled as an *NP* in the second sentence. The error is caused by the fact that *le traitement* from the second sentence (in *du traitement*, which is correctly analyzed as *de le traitement*) is an NP in a PP that depends on the noun *arrêt*. The parser that we use sometimes adds the information about the function of a phrase, this is the case in the first sentence here where *le traitement* is the object of the verb *arrêter*. This kind of examples suggests to put together similar node labels, such as NP and NP-OBJ. It would also be interesting to see whether some nodes are consistently similar in the parallel pairs, and hopefully find that those consistencies do not appear in pairs that should not be retained in a parallel corpus.

Let's analyze another typical example:

- *La prudence est recommandée chez les sujets atteints d'ulcères gastroduodénaux. (The vigilance is recommended in subjects suffering from gastroduodenal ulcers.)*

- *Ce médicament doit être utilisé avec prudence en cas d'ulcère de l'estomac ou du duodénum. (This medication must be used with vigilance in case of ulcers of the stomach and duodenum)*

There is only one pair of identical words here : *prudence (vigilance)*. This work is labelled as an NP in the first sentence and as a PP in the second sentence. The presence of *ulcère (ulcer)* in both sentences is not detected: the filter is currently looking for strictly identical words, while in these two sentences, *ulcère (ulcer)* occurs in its plural form in the first sentence and in its singular form in the second sentence. Hence, the filter must be more permissive in order to detect such occurrences. One solution is to work with a lemmatizer, another solution is to propose a more sophisticated word comparison function. This is a task where word embeddings could also be useful. We intend to test this possibility in future works.

Table 2 shows the results of classification with the different sentence pairs sets. For each experiment, the data were divided in two thirds for training and one third for testing. The results are reported by class (negative and positive) and positive class type (either equivalence or inclusion). The negative class has a perfect score in every metric because of the high degree of imbalance, the false negatives are not numerous enough to have an influence on the score. We can see that the syntactic method with a depth of exploration of three levels has a positive influence on precision, compared to unfiltered data, and recall is negatively impacted. We believe that being deprived of one third of such a small set of positive examples has a strong negative impact on performance. We should be able to improve recall if we prevent the positive examples from being filtered out, as we mentioned in the error analysis above. The results for inclusion show that this type of sentence pair is hard to recognize automatically. There is some improvement with filtered data, but the scores are low, especially recall. What we draw from those results is that the different sentence pairs types should be handled differently. It seems that we cannot expect to extract inclusion pairs in the same way as we extract equivalent pairs.

6. Conclusion

In this work, we proposed to address the problem of imbalance in the process of extracting parallel sentences from comparable corpora. We worked on a French comparable corpus made for biomedical text simplification. We showed that we could drastically reduce the number of negative examples (>98%) with simple heuristics and a syntactic comparison of sentence pairs, at the cost of losing some positive examples. Analyzing the errors, we showed that there were consistencies in what was left out and that should be kept, that can be addressed with improvements to the method, such as a better word comparison function and a more careful work on syntactic node label similarity. Even with those issues, we reduce the imbalance and improve precision on a classification task for equivalent sentences, thus reducing the manual work needed to check the output, which was the main objective. We also showed that inclusion pairs are much harder to process and that another method should be used for extracting that type.

7. Acknowledgements

We would like to thank the reviewers for their comments. This work was funded by the French National Agency for Research (ANR) as part of the *CLEAR* project (*Communication, Literacy, Education, Accessibility, Readability*), ANR-17-CE19-0016-01.

8. Bibliographical References

Bird, S., Klein, E., and Loper, E. (2009). *Natural Language Processing with Python*. O'Reilly Media, Inc., 1st edition.

Cardon, R. and Grabar, N. (2019). Parallel sentence retrieval from comparable corpora for biomedical text simplification. In *Proceedings of Recent Advances in Natural Language Processing*, pages 168–177, Varna, Bulgaria, september.

Deléger, L. and Zweigenbaum, P. (2009). Extracting lay paraphrases of specialized expressions from monolingual comparable medical corpora. In *Proceedings of the 2nd Workshop on Building and Using Comparable Corpora: from Parallel to Non-parallel Corpora (BUCC)*, pages 2–10, Singapore, August. Association for Computational Linguistics.

Duran, K., Rodriguez, J., and Bravo, M. (2014). Similarity of sentences through comparison of syntactic trees with pairs of similar words. In *11th International Conference on Electrical Engineering, Computing Science and Automatic Control (CCE)*, pages 1–6, Campeche, 09.

Grabar, N. and Cardon, R. (2018). CLEAR – Simple Corpus for Medical French. In *Workshop on Automatic Text Adaption (ATA)*, pages 1–11, Tilburg, Netherlands.

Jhamtani, H., Gangal, V., Hovy, E., and Nyberg, E. (2017). Shakespearizing modern language using copy-enriched sequence to sequence models. In *Proceedings of the Workshop on Stylistic Variation*, pages 10–19, Copenhagen, Denmark, September. Association for Computational Linguistics.

Kitaev, N. and Klein, D. (2018). Constituency parsing with a self-attentive encoder. In *Proceedings of the 56th Annual Meeting of the Association for Computational Linguistics (Volume 1: Long Papers)*, Melbourne, Australia, July. Association for Computational Linguistics.

Smith, J. R., Quirk, C., and Toutanova, K. (2010). Extracting parallel sentences from comparable corpora using document level alignment. In *Human Language Technologies: The 2010 Annual Conference of the North American Chapter of the Association for Computational Linguistics*, HLT '10, page 403–411, USA. Association for Computational Linguistics.

Xu, W., Callison-Burch, C., and Napoles, C. (2015). Problems in current text simplification research: New data can help. *Transactions of the Association for Computational Linguistics*, 3:283–297.

Zhang, Z. and Zweigenbaum, P. (2017). zNLP: Identifying parallel sentences in Chinese-English comparable corpora. In *Proceedings of the 10th Workshop on Building and Using Comparable Corpora*, pages 51–55, Vancouver, Canada, August. Association for Computational Linguistics.

Zweigenbaum, P., Sharoff, S., and Rapp, R. (2017). Overview of the second BUCC shared task: Spotting parallel sentences in comparable corpora. In *Proceedings of the 10th Workshop on Building and Using Comparable Corpora*, pages 60–67, Vancouver, Canada, August. Association for Computational Linguistics.

Proceedings of the 13th Workshop on Building and Using Comparable Corpora, pages 49–55
Language Resources and Evaluation Conference (LREC 2020), Marseille, 11–16 May 2020
© European Language Resources Association (ELRA), licensed under CC-BY-NC

LMU Bilingual Dictionary Induction System with Word Surface Similarity Scores for BUCC 2020

Silvia Severini[*], **Viktor Hangya**[*], **Alexander Fraser, Hinrich Schütze**
Center for Information and Language Processing
LMU Munich, Germany
{silvia, hangyav, fraser}@cis.uni-muenchen.de

Abstract

The task of Bilingual Dictionary Induction (BDI) consists of generating translations for source language words which is important in the framework of machine translation (MT). The aim of the BUCC 2020 shared task is to perform BDI on various language pairs using comparable corpora. In this paper, we present our approach to the task of English-German and English-Russian language pairs. Our system relies on Bilingual Word Embeddings (BWEs) which are often used for BDI when only a small seed lexicon is available making them particularly effective in a low-resource setting. On the other hand, they perform well on high frequency words only. In order to improve the performance on rare words as well, we combine BWE based word similarity with word surface similarity methods, such as orthography and transliteration information. In addition to the often used top-n translation method, we experiment with a margin based approach aiming for dynamic number of translations for each source word. We participate in both the open and closed tracks of the shared task and we show improved results of our method compared to simple vector similarity based approaches. Our system was ranked in the top-3 teams and achieved the best results for English-Russian.

Keywords: BDI, BWE, Orthography, Transliteration

1. Introduction

Bilingual Dictionary Induction is the task of inducing word translations from monolingual corpora in different languages. It has been studied extensively as it is one of the main tasks used for evaluating the quality of BWE models (Mikolov et al., 2013b; Vulic and Korhonen, 2016). It is also important for downstream tasks such as translating out-of-vocabulary words in MT (Huck et al., 2019).

Although there is a large amount of work for BDI, there is no standard way to measure the performance of the systems, the published results are not comparable and the pros and cons of the various approaches are not clear. The aim of the BUCC 2020 – *Bilingual Dictionary Induction from Comparable Corpora* – shared task (Rapp et al., 2020) is to solve this problem and compare various systems on a standard test set. It involves multiple language pairs including Chinese, English, French, German, Russian and Spanish and supports comparable monolingual corpora, and training and testing dictionaries for high, middle and low frequency words. In this paper, we present our approach to the shared task and show results on English-German and English-Russian.

BWEs are popular for solving BDI by calculating cosine similarity of word pairs and taking the n most similar candidates as translations for a given source word. They were shown to be very effective for the task using a small seed lexicon only (e.g., (Mikolov et al., 2013b)) as opposed to MT based approaches where parallel data is necessary. In addition, Conneau et al. (2018) and Artetxe et al. (2018) were able to learn BWEs without any seed dictionaries using a self-learning method that starts from an initial weak solution and improves the mapping iteratively. Due to this, BDI is one of the building blocks of unsupervised MT and are particularly relevant in low-resource settings (Artetxe et

al., 2019; Lample et al., 2018).

Although BWE based methods work well for translating high frequency words, it was shown that they tend to have low performance when translating low-frequency words or named entities due to poor vector representation of such words (Braune et al., 2018; Riley and Gildea, 2018; Czarnowska et al., 2019). By using character n-gram representations and Levenshtein similarity of words, Braune et al. (2018) showed improved results on rare and domain specific words. Similarly, Riley and Gildea (2018) improves the translation of such words by integrating orthographic information into the vector representation of words and in the mapping procedure of BWEs. On the other hand, these techniques are only applicable in the case of language pairs having the same scripts. Recently, Riley and Gildea (2020) proposed an unsupervised system based on expectation maximization and character-level RNN models to learn transliteration based similarity, i.e., edit distance similarity across different character sets. To train their system they took $5,000$ word pairs having the highest cosine similarity based on BWEs. However, this method could be noisy, since non-transliteration pairs could be generated as well.

In this paper, we present our approach to BDI focusing on the problems of low frequency words translation. We follow the approach of Braune et al. (2018) and improve low frequency translation by combining a BWE based model with other information coming from word surface similarity: orthography and transliteration. The orthographic model is used in the case of word pairs with shared alphabet and uses the Levenshtein similarity. The transliteration model is used for pairs with different scripts where an orthographic comparison would not be possible and it is obtained from our novel fully unsupervised transliteration model. In contrast to (Riley and Gildea, 2020), we propose a cleaning method for filtering non-transliteration pairs from the used dictionary before training the model to ensure a less noisy training

---

[*]The authors contributed equally to this manuscript.

signal.

We test our system on the *English-German* pairs (En-De, De-En) and *English-Russian* pairs (En-Ru, Ru-En) provided in the BUCC 2020 Shared Task (Rapp et al., 2020). We participate in both the open and closed tracks of the shared tasks, using embeddings extracted either from *Wikipedia* (Conneau et al., 2018) or *WaCKy* (Baroni et al., 2009) respectively. In addition to using a static number of most similar words as translation, we experimented with methods returning a dynamic number of translations given each source word.

In the rest of the paper, we first describe the approach and how we obtain the two word surface similarity scores. Then, we present the experiments on the BUCC 2020 dataset and discuss the results.

2. BUCC 2020 Shared Task

The BUCC 2020 Shared Task (Rapp et al., 2020) focuses on multilingual lexical knowledge extraction from comparable rather than from parallel corpora. It gives the opportunity to experiment with the BLI task providing corpora and bilingual datasets for different language pairs. It also provides training data and a common evaluation framework.

The shared task is divided into open and closed tracks. In the open track participants are allowed to use their own corpora and training data, whereas in the closed track they can use only the data provided by the organizers. This data includes monolingual corpora for each language which should be used for the mining of translations. Furthermore, the shared task provides training data that consists of tab-separated bilingual word pairs divided into high, medium and low frequency groups, i.e., words ranking in 5000 most frequent words, in the range of $5001 - 20000$ and $20001 - 50000$ respectively. The test sets are also split in the three groups, with 2000 words each. Both train and test are a subset of the MUSE dictionaries (Conneau et al., 2018) which were created using a Facebook internal translation tool. In addition they take the polysemy of words into account, meaning that some words have multiple translations. Due to this, the performance of the systems is determined by computing precision, recall and F_1 score[1] instead of *acc@n* used in other works (Vulic and Korhonen, 2016). For further information about the official data and setup we refer to the shared task description paper (Rapp et al., 2020).

3. Approach

To solve the BDI task we rely on both BWE and word surface based similarity. As in many related works, we calculate the vector similarity of words in order to find target language words having similar meaning compared to a given input word. However, BWEs tend to perform poorly when translating named entities and low-frequency words (Braune et al., 2018; Riley and Gildea, 2018). To alleviate the problem, we follow the approach of (Braune et al., 2018) and combine word similarity information from multiple BWE models and we look for similarly written source and target language words. The latter can be solved by looking for orthographically similar words in the case of English

---

[1] F_1 is the official score for system ranking.

and German. On the other hand, for English and Russian the approach is not applicable due to the different character sets of the two languages, thus we employ an unsupervised transliteration model.

3.1. Bilingual Word Embeddings

To build BWEs we follow the mapping approach of (Mikolov et al., 2013b), i.e., we build monolingual word embeddings (MWEs) which we then align to a share space using a seed dictionary. We create 4 types of MWE models for each language, since it was shown that combining them is beneficial for BDI (Braune et al., 2018): $\{word2vec, fasttext\} \times \{cbow, skipgram\}$ (Mikolov et al., 2013a; Bojanowski et al., 2017). We perform the mapping using *VecMap* (Artetxe et al., 2018) which learns an orthogonal projection of the source MWE to the target space. Although the approach supports unsupervised mapping, we use it in a supervised setup. As the seed lexicon, we use part of the provided high frequency dictionary. Although the dictionary contains multiple translations for some source words, we only use the first translation of each word in order to reduce noise. Finally, we generate a *similarity dictionary* based on each BWE type containing translation candidates, i.e., the 100 most similar target language words, for each source language word along with their similarity scores. We calculate the cosine similarity based *Cross-Domain Similarity Local Scaling* (CSLS) metric as the similarity score (Conneau et al., 2018) which adjusts the similarity values of a word based on the density of the area where it lies, i.e., it increases similarity values for a word lying in a sparse area and decreases values for a word in a dense area. In the simple case, word translation could be done by using the most similar target candidate for a given source word based on one of the dictionaries. On the other hand, our aim is to exploit the advantages of all BWE types which we achieve by ensembling the generated similarity dictionaries.

Ensembling   In order to merge various similarity dictionaries we follow a similar approach as (Braune et al., 2018). For this, we create a final similarity dictionary containing the 100 most similar target words for each source word along with their ensembled similarity scores which is given by:

$$Sim_e(S, T) = \mathcal{Q}_{i=1}^{M} \gamma_i Sim_i(S, T) \tag{1}$$

where S and T are the source and target words, $Sim_i(\cdot, \cdot)$ and γ_i is the similarity of two words based on the ith BWE type and its weight. As the $\mathcal{Q}$ function, we experimented with summing the weighted values or taking their maximum value. The former aims to emphasise candidates that are ranked high by multiple models while the latter takes the candidates in which a given model is confident. For simplicity we only calculate the score for target words that are in any of the dictionaries for a given source word instead of the full target language vocabulary. If a candidate word T is not in dictionary i we set $Sim_i(S, T)$ to 0. γ_i are tuned on the development set.

The above equation only requires dictionaries containing word pairs and their similarities allowing us to employ information from other sources as well, such as orthography and transliteration which we discuss in the following.

3.2. Orthographic Similarity

The translation of many words, such as named entities, numerical values, nationalities and loan words, are written similarly as the source word, thus we rely on orthographic similarity to improve the translation of such words. For English and German we follow the approach of (Braune et al., 2018) and use Levenshtein similarity, more precisely one minus the normalized Levenshtein distance, as the orthographic similarity of a given word pair. We generate similarity dictionaries as before but containing orthographically similar words, which we use as an additional element during ensembling. The generation of such a dictionary is computationally heavy, since each source word has to be compared to each word in the target language vocabulary leading to a large number of word pairs. Since most of the word pairs are not orthographically similar we follow the approach of Riley and Gildea (2018) to reduce the number of word pairs to compare. For this the *Symmetric Delete* algorithm is used, which takes as arguments a list of source words, target vocabulary and a constant k, and identifies all source-target word pairs that are identical after k insertions or deletions. We then calculate the Levenshtein similarity only for such word pairs.

3.3. Transliteration score

When dealing with word pairs from different scripts (i.e. En-Ru), we need a different measure of similarity because the alphabets are not shared. If we consider rare words, we know that many of them are transliterated (e.g., translated preserving the sound). Adam/Адам and Laura/Лаура are example of English-Russian transliteration pairs. Therefore, we propose a new method to capture similarities between words from different scripts through transliteration scores. In particular, we aim to improve the BWEs for rare and less frequent words incorporating the word scores coming from our transliteration model. The method is unsupervised given that we do not have transliteration pairs for training in the shared task setup – we have translation pairs, but they are not annotated as transliteration vs non-transliteration. The model is used in an unsupervised way to clean the training set and to get the final predictions. Our method consists of training a sequence-to-sequence model (Sutskever et al., 2014) on a "cleaned" set to get the transliteration scores. The model and the cleaning process are explained in the following.

3.3.1. Transliteration model

Once we cleaned the whole dataset as explained in the section below, we use it as the training set for our seq2seq model. The model works at the character-level and is made of an encoder and a decoder part with attention. They both contain multi-layered Gated Recurrent Units (Cho et al., 2014) but the encoder uses bidirectional GRUs that is able to encode both past and future context. The decoder exploits the "Global Attention" mechanism with the "dot" method of (Luong et al., 2015) to diminish the information loss of long sequences. The model has one encoder and one decoder layer with hidden size of 128. We use a dropout regularization probability of 0.1 and a learning rate of 0.01 with the SGD optimization algorithm.

Once the model is trained, we use it to calculate the negative log likelihood probability (pNLL) of each word in the target language vocabulary with respect to each test word because we saw that it was working better than the generation of transliteration words. In this way, we generated the similarity dictionary and we selected the 100 top scored words. Given a word pair $[S, T]$ with $t_1, .., t_N \in T$, we define the score as:

$$pNLL = \frac{(\sum_{i=1}^{N} nll(t_i)) + nll(EOS)}{N + 1} \qquad (2)$$

where $nll(t_i)$ is the Negative Log Likelihood probability of the ith character in T, and EOS is the "End Of String" token.

3.3.2. Cleaning process

The cleaning process aims to reduce the number of non-transliteration pairs in the initial dataset in an unsupervised way to better train the final transliteration model. The dataset is considered "cleaner" if it contains less non-transliteration pairs than the initial one and still enough transliteration pairs to allow the training of the model.

First, we randomly select 10 pairs that have a length difference greater than one as the "comparison set" and we fixed it for all the cleaning process. This length difference helps to find pairs that in most cases are not transliteration. We then carry out an iterative process. We split the dataset in training and test sets (80%-20%) and we train the character-level Encoder-Decoder model, explained in section 3.3.1 above, on the training set. The number of steps was chosen based on previous experiments. Then, we evaluate the test set on the model and we obtain a score for each test pair $(source, target)$. A score measures the negative log likelihood probability of predicting the target given the input. Higher scores mean higher probability for the input and target to be transliterations of each other. Then, we calculate the scores for the comparison set in the same way and we remove all the test pairs that are below the average score of the comparison set. Finally, we shuffle the training set with the remaining test pairs and we divide again in training and test. We repeat this process training a new model every time and cleaning the test set for a fixed number of iterations found experimentally,

The dataset has been divided into low, medium and high-frequency pairs. We exploited this fact with the assumption that the low-frequency set should contain rare words and more nouns, so consequently more transliteration pairs than the high-frequency set. Therefore, we first clean the low set with the iterative process. Then, we mix the cleaned low set with the uncleaned medium set and run the process on it. Finally, we mix the result of this process with the high-frequency set and run the last iterative method to get the cleaned dataset that we used in the final transliteration model. Note that we only rely on the training portion of the released high, medium and low dictionaries (see Section 4).

3.4. Dynamic Translation

BDI is often performed by returning the top-1 or top-5 most probable translations of a source word (Mikolov et al., 2013b). Since the dictionaries of the shared task contain a dynamic number of translations, the participants had to decide the number of words to return. During our experiments we found that using top-1 translation for the low and middle and top-2 for high frequency sets gives consistent results thus we used this solution as our official submission. However, we experimented with dynamic methods as well. Based on the manual investigation of the ensembled word pair similarity scores, we found that having a global threshold value would not be sufficient for selecting multiple translations for a given source word, since the similarity values of the top-1 translations have a large deviation across source words. This is also known as the hubness problem (Dinu and Baroni, 2014), i.e., the vector representation of some words tend to lie in high density regions, thus have high similarity to a large number of words, while others lie in low density regions having low scores. Instead of using a global threshold value, we followed the margin based approach proposed by (Artetxe and Schwenk, 2019) for parallel sentence mining which in a sense calculates a local threshold value for each source word. We adapt this method for BDI and calculate a score of each candidate word T for a given source word S by:

$$score(S, T) = margin(Sim_e(S, T), avg(S)) \quad (3)$$

where $avg(S)$ is the average similarity scores of S and the 100 most similar candidates based on the ensemble scores $Sim_e(\cdot, \cdot)$. We experimented with two variants of the $margin$ function:

$$marginDistance(x, y) = x - y \quad (4)$$

$$marginRatio(x, y) = \frac{x}{y} \quad (5)$$

The aim of both methods is to normalize the similarities based on the averaged similarity values so that a global threshold value can be used to select translations. The former method calculates the distance between the similarity value of the target candidate and the averaged similarity while the latter calculates their ratio. Finally, we consider each target candidate of a given source word as translation if its score is higher than the threshold value. We tune one threshold value for each language pair and word frequency category using the development sets. In addition, since each source word should have at least one translation, we always consider the top-1 most similar candidate to be a translation.

4. Experimental Setup

We submitted BDI outputs for both the closed and open tracks which differ only in the used BWEs. For the closed track we only relied on the released monolingual corpora and training dictionaries. For the MWEs we used the *WaCKy* corpora (Baroni et al., 2009) and built *word2vec* cbow and skipgram models (Mikolov et al., 2013a), and *fasttext* cbow models (Bojanowski et al., 2017), while we used the released fasttext skipgram models from the shared task website. We used the same parameters used by the organizers for both methods: minimum word count 30; vector dimension 300; context window size 7; number of negatives

sampled 10 and in addition, number of epochs 10 for fasttext. To align MWEs of the same type, we used *VecMap* (Artetxe et al., 2018) in a supervised setup. As the training signal we used the official shared task dictionaries which are a subset of the *MUSE* dictionaries released in (Conneau et al., 2018). We split them into train, development and test sets $(70\%/15\%/15\%)^2$ which we used for training BWEs and the transliteration model, tuning parameters and reporting final results respectively. Since we tuned various parameters, such as ensembling weights or threshold values for margin based translation, for each language pair and frequency category, we do not report each value here but discuss them in the following section. For the generation of BWE based similarity dictionaries we only considered the most frequent $200K$ words when calculating CSLS similarities as in (Conneau et al., 2018). We experimented with larger vocabulary sizes but achieved lower scores. In contrast, for the orthography and transliteration based dictionaries we considered all words in the monolingual corpora which have at least frequency 5^3.

For the open track we followed the same approach as above but instead of using WaCKy based MWEs we used pre-trained Wikipedia based monolingual fasttext skipgram models similarly as in (Conneau et al., 2018). Although we use only one type of BWE model (instead of four) in addition to the orthography or transliteration based similarities we achieved higher performance especially for the middle and low frequency sets.

5. Results

As the official evaluation metric of the shared task we present F_1 scores of our approach. We compare multiple systems to show the effects of various modules of our approach on our test splits in Table 1. We compare systems using only one similarity dictionary using either fasttext (FTT) cbow or surface similarity and our complete system ensembling five similarity dictionaries using tuned weights (two for the open track). We also show results of our open track submission (Wiki). All systems return top-n translations except *ensemble + margin*. We used $n = 1$ for the low and middle frequency sets and also for Ru-En high, while for the rest $n = 2$ gave the best results. When using margin based translation, we show the best performing method based on the development set which we discuss in more details below. In general, it can be seen that in our closed track submission the best results were achieved by ensembling various information from different sources. The BWE based model achieved fairly good results for the high and middle frequency sets but often lower results than the surface similarity based model for low frequency words. On the contrary, the surface based systems performed well as the frequency of words decreases, having low scores for the high set. Based on investigation of the test splits, not surprisingly the results correlate with the number of words that are written similarly on both the source and target language sides showing the importance of this module during BDI.

---

[2] We kept all translations of a given source word in the same set.

[3] Additionally, we filtered words that contained at least 2 consecutive punctuation marks or numbers.

| | High | | | |
	En-De	De-En	En-Ru	Ru-En
FTT cbow	38.17	46.37	33.52	46.78
Surface	4.31	3.41	7.38	14.64
Ensemble	40.59	49.56	38.33	54.12
Ensemble + Margin	39.76	49.90	36.23	54.71
Wiki	41.40	48.61	39.43	54.90

| | Middle | | | |
	En-De	De-En	En-Ru	Ru-En
FTT cbow	30.62	36.00	20.14	39.82
Surface	7.76	10.11	13.47	16.93
Ensemble	47.76	51.71	33.24	49.64
Ensemble + Margin	47.76	51.89	36.17	49.72
Wiki	49.18	53.66	43.55	56.53

| | Low | | | |
	En-De	De-En	En-Ru	Ru-En
FTT cbow	24.19	33.05	15.03	21.53
Surface	24.62	20.12	20.62	30.25
Ensemble	63.82	69.41	30.11	42.99
Ensemble + Margin	63.82	69.41	30.50	43.17
Wiki	65.14	73.10	51.72	57.01

Table 1: F_1 scores for English-German and English-Russian language pairs in both directions and the three frequency categories on our test split. The first two models use either a dictionary based on embeddings or surface similarity while the rest combines all of the available (two for Wiki and five for the rest). Ensemble + Margin shows results with dynamic number of translations per source words using the best margin based method and top-n ($n \in \{1, 2\}$) is applied for the rest. Wiki shows our open track submission.

By looking at the ensembling scores, the BWE and surface scores seem additive showing that the two methods extend each other, i.e., the source word could be translated with either of the models.

Model weights   As mentioned, we tuned our system parameters on the development set. Without presenting the large number of parameters, we detail our conclusions. Comparing the usefulness of the BWE types we found similarly to (Braune et al., 2018) that fasttext models are more important by handling morphological variation of words better due to relying on character n-grams which is especially important for Russian. On the other hand, word2vec models also got significant weights showing their additional positive effect on the results. Comparing skipgram and cbow models we found that the weights of fasttext cbow and fasttext skipgram are similar (the former has a bit higher weight) while word2vec cbow got close to zero weight, only the word2vec skipgram model is effective. The weights of the surface based similarity dictionaries were lowest for the high frequency sets and higher for the other two, but counter intuitively it was the highest for the middle set 3 out of 4 times. The reason for this is that many words in the low sets are not included in the most frequent $200K$ words that we used in the BWEs but in the surface dictionaries only, thus independent of the weights the translation is based on the latter. On the other hand, many source words have similarly written pairs on the target side even though they have proper translations, e.g., source: *ambulance*; transliteration: *амбуланс*; translation: *скорая*, thus having high weight led to incorrect translations. As mentioned in Section 3 we experimented with summing the scores in the dictionaries during ensembling or taking their maximum. The former consistently performed better for En-De and De-En while the latter performed better for En-Ru and Ru-En. The reason lies in the different surface models: orthographic similarity for German and transliteration for Russian.

Dynamic translation   The ensemble+margin system shows our results with the system predicting a dynamic number of words as translation based on the margin method. We tuned the threshold value for both *marginDistance* and *marginRatio* and show the best performing setup. We achieved some improvements in most of the cases compared to ensemble with top-n, except for En-De high and En-Ru high. On the other hand, we achieved significant improvements for En-Ru middle and Ru-En low. However, we found that this method is not robust in various scenarios since the best parameters (margin method variation and threshold value) were different across our test sets and we found no pattern in them, e.g., high threshold for low frequency sets and low value for higher frequencies. On the other hand, top-1 and top-2 translations performed more consistently. We expect the margin based method to perform better than top-n for mixed frequency test set.

Open Track   In our open track submission we ensembled Wikipedia based fasttext skipgram based BWEs with surface information. Although our system relied only on the two similarity models we achieved significant improvements compared to our closed track systems, especially for En-Ru and Ru-En. The reason for this lies in the number of OOVs in the BWE vocabularies. As mentioned we used the $200K$ most frequent word for both WaCKy and Wikipedia based BWEs but for the former more source test words are OOVs. We investigated the gold translations as well and found a similar trend, i.e., there are more cases for the closed track models where the source word's embedding is known but not that of its gold translation. Our conjecture is that the machine translation system used for the creation of the MUSE dictionaries relies more on Wikipedia texts, thus these models perform better on these test sets.

Manual analysis   In table 2 we show interesting samples taken from test set results that we created out of the training data provided. The last two columns show the top predictions according to BWE based scores, and orthographic or transliteration scores. The Surface column is chosen as the final prediction when no translation is provided for the source word meaning that the source is not present in the BWEs. This helps to solve OOV word issues. We can see that the surface prediction is also useful for source words that are not proper names like in the *[polarität, polarity]* example. The last two rows show negative results where the ensembling led to incorrect predictions. The *[бартольд, barthold]* sample shows an incorrect weighting of the final prediction which for example could have been solved with a local weighting that could adjust the importance of the

Source	Gold	Ensemble	FTT cbow	Surface
фейерверки	fireworks	fireworks	**fireworks**	feierwerk
левандовский	levandovski	levandovski	/	**levandovski**
workouts	тренировки	тренировки	**тренировки**	воркуты
hippocrates	гиппократ	гиппократ	**гиппократ**	покравительство
massimiliano	массимилиано	массимилиано	/	**массимилиано**
bolschoi	bolshoi	bolshoi	/	**bolshoi**
nikotin	nicotine	nicotine	alcohol	**nicotine**
polarität	polarity	polarity	polarities	**polarity**
бартольд	barthold	ismaili	ismaili	**barthold**
inedible	ungenießbar	incredible	**ungenießbar**	incredible

Table 2: Samples from our test set. The *Ensemble* column contains the output of our complete system, *FTT cbow* contains the output based on FTT only, and *Surface* column contains the output based on the orthographic or transliteration similarity scores. In bold there are the correct predictions in the last two columns. The slash "/" symbol indicates that the source word is not in the embedding vocabulary. The last two samples are cases where the ensemble model selected the final prediction wrongly.

	High			
	En-De	De-En	En-Ru	Ru-En
Closed	41.7	46.8	39.4	54.2
Open	42.0	46.6	38.2	56.2

	Middle			
	En-De	De-En	En-Ru	Ru-En
Closed	45.6	53.8	34.4	51.5
Open	47.9	57.9	40.4	56.9

	Low			
	En-De	De-En	En-Ru	Ru-En
Closed	66.0	69.2	29.9	41.4
Open	67.1	72.9	49.2	58.4

Table 3: Official BUCC 2020 results of our closed and open track submissions.

BWEs and transliteration based on the candidate scores. The last sample is incorrect probably because of the strong similarity between the source word and the orthography top prediction. We also have noise issues in this case (i.e., "incredible" is not a German word) that could be solved with a language detection based filtering.

Official results We show the performance of our submissions in the official shared task evaluation in table 3. Overall, our system was ranked in the top 3 teams and it achieved top 1 results on the English and Russian language pairs. As mentioned above our closed track submission involved the ensembling of BWE and word surface similarity scores and taking either top-1 or top-2 translations based on the frequency set. The open track submission differs only in the used word embeddings, e.i., we used pre-trained wikipedia fasttext skipgram embeddings only. Our official results are similar to the results on our test splits in table 1 which indicates the robustness of our approach.

6. Conclusion

Bilingual dictionary induction is an important task for many cross-lingual applications. In this paper we presented our approach to the BUCC 2020 which is the first shared task on BDI aiming to compare various systems in a unified framework on multiple language pairs. We followed a BWE based approach focusing of low frequency words by improving their translations using surface similarity measures.

For our English-German system we used orthographic similarity. Since for the English-Russian language pair orthography is not applicable due to different scripts, we introduced a novel character RNN based transliteration model. We trained this system on the shared task training dictionary which we cleaned by filtering non-transliteration pairs. In our results we showed improvements compared to a simple BWE based baseline for high, medium and low frequency test sets. We showed that by using multiple BWE types better performance can be reached on the high set. Furthermore, the medium and low sets surface similarity gave significant performance improvements. In addition to translating words to their top-1 or top-2 most similar candidates, we experimented with a margin based dynamic method which showed further improvements. On the other hand, since we found that it is not robust across the various setups, we used top-n translations in our official submission. Based on the analysis of our results, future improvement directions are better combinations of various similarity dictionaries, such as source word based local weighting, getting rid of the seed dictionary in the overall method, and a more robust dynamic prediction approach.

Acknowledgements

We gratefully acknowledge funding for this work by the European Research Council (ERC) under the European Union's Horizon 2020 research and innovation programme (grant agreements № 640550 and № 740516).

Bibliographical References

Artetxe, M. and Schwenk, H. (2019). Margin-based Parallel Corpus Mining with Multilingual Sentence Embeddings. In *Proceedings of the 57th Annual Meeting of the Association for Computational Linguistics*, pages 3197–3203.

Artetxe, M., Labaka, G., and Agirre, E. (2018). A robust self-learning method for fully unsupervised cross-lingual mappings of word embeddings. In *Proceedings of the 56th Annual Meeting of the Association for Computational Linguistics (Volume 1: Long Papers)*, pages 789–798.

Artetxe, M., Labaka, G., and Agirre, E. (2019). An Effective Approach to Unsupervised Machine Translation. In *Proceedings of the 57th Annual Meeting of the Association for Computational Linguistics*, pages 194–203.

Baroni, M., Bernardini, S., Ferraresi, A., and Zanchetta, E. (2009). The wacky wide web: a collection of very large linguistically processed web-crawled corpora. *Language resources and evaluation*, 43(3):209–226.

Bojanowski, P., Grave, E., Joulin, A., and Mikolov, T. (2017). Enriching Word Vectors with Subword Information. *Transactions of the Association for Computational Linguistics*, 5:135–146.

Braune, F., Hangya, V., Eder, T., and Fraser, A. (2018). Evaluating bilingual word embeddings on the long tail. In *Proceedings of the 2018 Conference of the North American Chapter of the Association for Computational Linguistics: Human Language Technologies, Volume 2 (Short Papers)*, pages 188–193.

Cho, K., Van Merriënboer, B., Gulcehre, C., Bahdanau, D., Bougares, F., Schwenk, H., and Bengio, Y. (2014). Learning phrase representations using rnn encoder-decoder for statistical machine translation. In *Proceedings of the 2014 Conference on Empirical Methods in Natural Language Processing (EMNLP)*, pages 1724–1734.

Conneau, A., Lample, G., Ranzato, M., Denoyer, L., and Jégou, H. (2018). Word Translation Without Parallel Data. In *Proceedings of the International Conference on Learning Representations*, pages 1–14.

Czarnowska, P., Ruder, S., Grave, E., Cotterell, R., and Copestake, A. (2019). Don't Forget the Long Tail! A Comprehensive Analysis of Morphological Generalization in Bilingual Lexicon Induction. In *Proceedings of the 2019 Conference on Empirical Methods in Natural Language Processing and the 9th International Joint Conference on Natural Language Processing (EMNLP-IJCNLP)*, pages 974–983.

Dinu, G. and Baroni, M. (2014). Improving zero-shot learning by mitigating the hubness problem. *CoRR*, abs/1412.6568.

Huck, M., Hangya, V., and Fraser, A. (2019). Better OOV Translation with Bilingual Terminology Mining. In *Proceedings of the 57th Annual Meeting of the Association for Computational Linguistics*, pages 5809–5815.

Lample, G., Ott, M., Conneau, A., Denoyer, L., and Ranzato, M. (2018). Phrase-Based & Neural Unsupervised Machine Translation. In *Proceedings of the 2018 Conference on Empirical Methods in Natural Language Processing*, pages 5039–5049.

Luong, M.-T., Pham, H., and Manning, C. D. (2015). Effective approaches to attention-based neural machine translation. In *Proceedings of the 2015 Conference on Empirical Methods in Natural Language Processing*, pages 1412–1421.

Mikolov, T., Chen, K., Corrado, G., and Dean, J. (2013a). Efficient estimation of word representations in vector space. In *Proceedings of the International Conference on Learning Representations*.

Mikolov, T., Le, Q. V., and Sutskever, I. (2013b). Exploiting Similarities among Languages for Machine Translation. *CoRR*, abs/1309.4.

Rapp, R., Zweigenbaum, P., and Sharoff, S. (2020). Overview of the fourth BUCC shared task: bilingual dictionary extraction from comparable corpora. In *Proceedings of the 13th Workshop on Building and Using Comparable Corpora*, pages 1–6.

Riley, P. and Gildea, D. (2018). Orthographic Features for Bilingual Lexicon Induction. In *Proceedings of the 56th Annual Meeting of the Association for Computational Linguistics (Volume 1: Long Papers)*, page 390–394.

Riley, P. and Gildea, D. (2020). Unsupervised bilingual lexicon induction across writing systems. *arXiv preprint arXiv:2002.00037*.

Sutskever, I., Vinyals, O., and Le, Q. V. (2014). Sequence to sequence learning with neural networks. In *Advances in neural information processing systems*, pages 3104–3112.

Vulic, I. and Korhonen, A. (2016). On the Role of Seed Lexicons in Learning Bilingual Word Embeddings. In *Proceedings of the 54th Annual Meeting of the Association for Computational Linguistics*, pages 247–257.

Proceedings of the 13th Workshop on Building and Using Comparable Corpora, pages 56–60
Language Resources and Evaluation Conference (LREC 2020), Marseille, 11–16 May 2020

TALN/LS2N Participation at the BUCC Shared Task:
Bilingual Dictionary Induction from Comparable Corpora

Martin Laville, Amir Hazem and Emmanuel Morin
LS2N, UMR CNRS 6004, Université de Nantes, France
firstname.lastname@ls2n.fr

Abstract

This paper describes the TALN/LS2N system participation at the Building and Using Comparable Corpora (BUCC) shared task. We first introduce three strategies: (i) a word embedding approach based on fastText embeddings; (ii) a concatenation approach using both character Skip-gram and character CBOW models, and finally (iii) a cognates matching approach based on an exact match string similarity. Then, we present the applied strategy for the shared task which consists in the combination of the embeddings concatenation and the cognates matching approaches. The covered languages are French, English, German, Russian and Spanish. Overall, our system mixing embeddings concatenation and perfect cognates matching obtained the best results while compared to individual strategies, except for English-Russian and Russian-English language pairs for which the concatenation approach was preferred.

Keywords: Bilingual lexicon induction, Comparable corpora, Cognates, Word embeddings

1. Introduction

Cross-lingual word embeddings learning has triggered great attention in the recent years and several bilingual supervised (Mikolov et al., 2013; Xing et al., 2015; Artetxe et al., 2018a) and unsupervised (Artetxe et al., 2018b; Conneau et al., 2017) alignment methods have been proposed so far. Also, multilingual alignment approaches which consists in mapping several languages in one common space via a pivot language (Smith et al., 2017) or by training all language pairs simultaneously (Chen and Cardie, 2018; Wada et al., 2019; Taitelbaum et al., 2019b; Taitelbaum et al., 2019a; Alaux et al., 2018) are attracting a great attention.

Among possible downstream applications of cross-lingual embedding models: Bilingual Lexicon Induction (BLI) which consists in the identification of translation pairs based on a comparable corpus. The BUCC shared task offers the first evaluation framework on BLI from comparable corpora. It covers six languages (English, French, German, Russian, Spanish and Chinese) and two corpora (Wikipedia and WaCKy). We describe in this paper our participation at the BLI shared task. We start by evaluating the cross-lingual word embedding mapping approach (VecMap) (Artetxe et al., 2018a) using fastText embeddings. Then, we present an extension of VecMap approach that uses the concatenation of two mapped embedding models (Hazem and Morin, 2018). Finally, we present a cognates matching approach, merely an exact match string similarity.

Based on the obtained results of the studied approaches, we derive our proposed system –Mix (Conc + Dist)– which combines the outputs of the embeddings concatenation and the cognates matching approaches. Overall, the obtained results on the validation data sets are in favor of our system for all language pairs except for English-Russian and Russian-English pairs, where the cognates matching approach obviously showed very weak results and for which the concatenation approach was preferred.

In the following, Section 2 describes the shared task data

sets, Section 3 presents the tested approaches and the chosen strategy. The results are given in Section 4, Section 5 discusses the quality of the seed lexicons, and finally, Section 6 concludes our work.

2. BLI Shared Task

The topic of the shared task is bilingual lexicon induction from comparable corpora. Its aim is to extract for each given source word, its target translations. The quality of the extracted lexicons is measured in terms of F1-score. To allow a deeper results analysis, the evaluation is conducted on three test sets corresponding to frequency ranges of the source language word: high (the frequency is among the 5000 most frequent words), mid (words ranking between 5001 and 20000) and low (words ranking between 20001 to 50000).

2.1. Tracks

The BLI shared task is composed of two tracks that is: (i) the closed task and (ii) the open task. In the closed task, only the data sets provided by the organizers can be used, while in the open track, external data as well as other language pairs evaluation are allowed. In this paper, only the closed track is addressed.

2.2. Data Sets

Two comparable corpora are provided: Wikipedia and WaCKy corpora (Baroni et al., 2009). Following the recommendations of the organizers, Table 1 illustrates the language pairs and their corresponding corpora that we address in the closed track.

Language	*de*	*es*	*fr*	*ru*
en	WaCKy	Wikipedia	WaCKy	WaCKy
de	-	-	WaCKy	-

Table 1: Corpus used for every language pair

Our training seed lexicons are from Conneau et al. (2017), for the validation results, we split these lists 80/20.

3. Approach

In this section, we present the three tested strategies as well as the chosen system to address the BLI shared task.

3.1. Word Embeddings and Mapping

To extract bilingual lexicons from comparable corpora, a well-known word embedding approach that maps source words in a target space has been introduced (Mikolov et al., 2013) and several mapping improvements have been proposed (Xing et al., 2015; Artetxe et al., 2018a). The basic idea is to learn an efficient transfer matrix that preserves translation pairs proximity of a seed lexicon. After the mapping step, a similarity measure is used to rank the translation candidates.

To apply the mapping approach, several embedding models can be used such as Skip-gram and CBOW (Mikolov et al., 2013), Glove (Pennington et al., 2014), character Skip-gram (Bojanowski et al., 2016), etc. In our approach, we used fastText (Bojanowski et al., 2016) as our word embeddings representations. We trained character Skip-gram and CBOW models, using the same parameters as the given pre-trained embeddings for both methods: minCount: 30; dim: 300; ws (context window): 7; epochs: 10; neg (number of negatives sampled): 10. For the English-Spanish pair, our embeddings were trained on Wikipedia. For all the other language pairs, the embedding models were trained on their corresponding WaCKy corpora.

After training our embeddings, we used the VecMap tool from Artetxe et al. (2018a) to project by pairs every source embeddings space in its corresponding target space (i.e. Skip-gram English mapped with Skip-gram Spanish or CBOW French mapped with CBOW German). We used the supervised method and split the training seed lexicon 80/20 for training and validation. For the submitted results, we took the whole seed lexicon as training for the mapping. Once our embeddings were projected in the same space, we compared every source word of our reference lists to every target word of the vocabulary with a similarity measure. We used the CSLS (Conneau et al., 2017), which is based on the cosine similarity but reduces the similarity for word vectors in dense areas and increases it for isolated ones:

$$CSLS(x_s, y_t) = 2cos(x_s, y_t) - knn(x_s) - knn(y_t) \quad (1)$$

where x_s (y_t) is the vector from source (target) space and $knn(x_s)$ ($knn(y_t)$) is the mean of the cosine of its k-nearest neighbors in the target (source) space.

This similarity measure allows us to order the target words from the most to the less likely to be the translation, but as there is multiple words as valid translations, we can not just keep the first word of each ranking. We used two criteria to select the candidates from the embeddings approach: i) a maximal number of candidates that we want to keep for each source word and ii) a minimal CSLS value to validate the candidates. We present the different values that we used for every language pair in Table 2. These values were fixed empirically on the validation set.

Language pair	Cand. $\leq$	Sim. $\geq$
en-es	4	0.1
es-en	2	0.08
en-de	5	0.06
de-en	5	0.04
en-fr	3	0.08
fr-en	2	0.04
en-ru	4	0.05
ru-en	2	0.03
de-fr	2	0.08
fr-de	2	0.06

Table 2: Parameters for selection of candidates for every language pair

3.2. Embeddings Concatenation

In order to take advantage of several embedding models, Hazem and Morin (2018) proposed an extension of the mapping approach by applying the concatenation or addition of two embedding models before performing the mapping approach. In our case, and for each language, we applied the concatenation of character CBOW and character Skip-gram models for each word. Starting from the mapped 300 dimensional embeddings from the previous step, we obtained a concatenated embedding vector of 600 dimensions for each source and target words.

3.3. Perfect Cognates

A careful analysis of the training reference lists revealed that many translation pairs were graphically identical, especially for the low frequency lists. While some of these words are perfect cognates, a part of them are inconsistencies (i.e. the English to French translation pair *someone - someone*). We give more details of these problems in Section 5. To take this into consideration, we selected as valid candidates for every source word its perfect cognates if present in the target vocabulary. We added the constraint that each translation word pairs must have a distribution with a proportional factor of n. Given a source word w_s and its corresponding translation w_t, and given the frequency of w_s ($freq(w_s)$), respectively the frequency of w_t ($freq(w_t)$). The constraint is represented as:

$$\frac{1}{n} \leq \frac{freq(w_s)}{freq(w_t)} \leq n \quad (2)$$

where n was fixed empirically to 100.

3.4. Mixing the Candidates

To improve performance, combining several approaches is often performed. As will be shown in Table 3 of the results Section, the embeddings approach performs better on high frequency pairs while the perfect cognates method shows good results on lower range pairs. Hence, we naturally combined the extracted candidates of both strategies to provide one final mixed list, without taking into account previous limit of the number of candidates. This mixing approach also noted –Mix (Conc + Dist)–, corresponds to our participating system to the BLI shared task. One exception however, concerns English and Russian languages for which we applied the concatenation approach only.

Frequency	en-es				es-en			
	high	mid	low	all	high	mid	low	all
Skip-gram	60.1	62.8	57.2	60.4	62.5	64.2	65.9	63.9
CBOW	57.1	56.8	54.1	56.4	59.7	60.2	56.2	59.0
Concatenation	60.9	**64.5**	62.8	62.4	62.6	65.5	65.3	64.3
Perfect Cognates	23.3	37.5	63.3	38.3	22.8	37.8	65.4	40.9
Mix (Conc + Dist)	**61.0**	61.8	**74.4**	**64.3**	**63.5**	**68.6**	**79.1**	**69.5**

Frequency	en-de				de-en			
	high	mid	low	all	high	mid	low	all
Skip-gram	47.6	43.6	29.8	43.4	50.6	47.6	33.7	45.8
CBOW	43.4	41.4	23.0	39.6	45.5	43.9	31.6	41.8
Concatenation	47.9	45.2	30.8	44.3	50.8	50.0	34.0	46.7
Perfect Cognates	21.1	35.6	67.8	37.2	24.1	35.7	69.9	41.2
Mix (Conc + Dist)	**50.9**	**55.0**	**71.8**	**56.4**	**57.2**	**62.3**	**72.9**	**63.1**

Frequency	en-fr				fr-en			
	high	mid	low	all	high	mid	low	all
Skip-gram	56.5	45.7	31.8	48.0	60.2	49.1	30.3	49.7
CBOW	51.4	42.0	31.1	44.1	58.5	48.7	29.4	48.4
Concatenation	57.8	45.8	34.6	49.3	62.8	55.4	36.2	54.0
Perfect Cognates	27.2	42.7	74.6	45.6	32.5	51.9	75.0	52.0
Mix (Conc + Dist)	**60.6**	**60.4**	**80.3**	**65.2**	**66.5**	**68.1**	**78.5**	**70.4**

Frequency	en-ru				ru-en			
	high	mid	low	all	high	mid	low	all
Skip-gram	41.3	31.7	13.2	34.0	53.8	40.6	20.7	41.9
CBOW	40.6	28.2	13.7	32.8	49.5	39.5	19.1	39.3
Concatenation	**42.6**	**32.6**	14.4	**35.3**	**55.5**	**44.3**	**22.8**	**44.4**
Perfect Cognates	7.4	6.6	13.2	8.6	0.0	0.0	0.0	0.0
Mix (Conc + Dist)	42.3	29.9	**21.0**	34.5	-	-	-	-

Frequency	de-fr				fr-de			
	high	mid	low	all	high	mid	low	all
Skip-gram	58.3	41.9	17.4	43.1	56.2	44.0	12.3	42.4
CBOW	52.7	32.7	14.4	36.6	51.2	39.9	11.7	38.5
Concatenation	60.2	44.2	17.9	44.6	56.8	46.9	14.9	44.2
Perfect Cognates	43.4	72.2	82.9	67.4	41.5	68.3	86.9	67.4
Mix (Conc + Dist)	**67.9**	**78.8**	**85.5**	**77.0**	**62.9**	**74.7**	**87.7**	**74.0**

Table 3: F1-score for our different approaches and language pairs

4. Results

Table 3 presents the obtained results (F1-score) of the individual strategies: (i) the mapping approach (Skip-gram and CBOW); (ii) the concatenation approach (Concatenation); (iii) the perfect cognates approach; and our proposed system (iv) Mix (Conc + Dist), on the validation sets for all language pairs.

We notice that mixing the candidates from the concatenated embeddings method and the perfect cognates extraction (Mix (Conc + Dist)) obtains the best results in almost every configuration, except one from English to Spanish and, obviously, the two pairs containing Russian, due to the different alphabets between English and Russian. Nevertheless, the English to Russian pair has a F1-score superior to zero, meaning that some Russian words are not written in Cyrillic, questioning the consistency of the lists.

The better results of the mixed method indicate a good complementarity of both approaches, which is confirmed by the trends regarding the frequency lists. We observe that the embeddings approach performs better on high frequency pairs and then degrades as the frequency decreases. Conversely, for the perfect cognates approach, the results are very high for the low frequency pairs and degrades for translation pairs of higher frequencies. The decline of results for perfect cognates is mostly due to the fact that high frequency words tend to have more translations than low ones (see Table 4) and the perfect cognates can at most predict one translation per source word.

The numbers illustrated in Table 4 corresponds to the validation lists, and not to the whole dictionaries.

As additional information, not shown in Table 3, it is to note that the perfect cognates method has a high precision for most language pairs, and it finds usually for more than half of the source words a perfect cognate in the target vocabulary. And thus, the results in F1-score are particularly high for the German-French pair in both directions as only few source words have more than one translation on the reference lists (1.03 target words per source words).

Finally, we note that the embeddings approach for the English-Spanish pair in both directions presents way better

Language pair	high	mid	low	all
en-es	2.34	1.58	1.10	1.67
en-de	2.83	1.81	1.14	1.93
fr-en	1.64	1.42	1.15	1.40
de-fr	1.08	1.02	1.00	1.03

Table 4: Ratio of target words per source words for the validation lists for some language pair on different lists

results than other language pairs (10 to almost 30 points). Unlike other pairs trained on WaCKy, this pair is the only one trained on Wikipedia, contradicting the idea that "the WaCKy corpora seem somewhat better suited for the dictionary induction task than Wikipedia". To verify this statement, we used pre-trained word embeddings from Grave et al. (2018) to check if the corpus was really the main problem. And actually, using the pre-trained embeddings on Wikipedia or Common Crawl led to much better results than the results obtained using the WaCKy corpora, reaching about the same F1-score as the English-Spanish language pair.

Our final results for the shared task were reported from the mixed approach for all language pairs but the two with Russian, for which we only took the results from the concatenation approach.

5. Seed Lexicon Analysis

As mentioned in the shared task, we report here the problems found in the seed lexicon.

We first noticed the presence of graphically identical pairs on the English-Russian pair, whereas the two languages have a different alphabet. This results are visible in Table 3 at the Perfect Cognates corresponding list. These instances are only present on the English to Russian language pair, suggesting a better control has been done for the source part of the lists.

A brief inspection of the lists makes us notice the presence of multiple words not belonging to the language of interest (i.e. on the French part of the English to French seed lexicon: *grammy, gov, god, northwest, phoenix* and many others) and we suggest the usage of monolingual dictionary to get rid of them. We even find pairs with none of the words belonging to one of the two languages (in the German to French seed lexicon the pair *times - times*, which should be *zeit - temps* if we translate it from English, or *ram - ram* instead of *ramm - bélier*).

We also observe many proper names and while some of them can be interesting to translate, most of them are graphically identical words (*jura, edward, lille...* on French to German or *calais, guanajuato...* on English to French), and we question the utility of translating such words, especially when some of them are not correctly presented (the German to French seed lexicon proposes a *mans - mans* pair, and we assume this is an incomplete form of the city "Le Mans" in France).

Focusing on the French part of some lists, we notice inconsistency with the use of diacritics (i.e. é, è...), the word *events* in English has four proposed translations in French, each being a variation of accents: *évènements, evénements,*
evenements, and *événements*. While in French, both *é* or *è* are accepted for the second *e*, the first one should always be an *é*. The English word *development* being another example with *developpement* and *développement* while only the latter should be a correct translation.

Still on the French part, we notice that the inflectional morphology also suffers from incoherence. In the German to French pair, *allein* is only translated with its masculine (*seul*) and feminine (*seule*) and not its plural forms (*seuls* and *seules*), but *ausgebildet* translations are only *formés* and *formé*, forgetting the feminine forms. We add that in the English to French pair *christian* being translated to *chrétiens, chrétienne, chrétien* (and *christian*, which can only be a proper name in French) instead of *chrétiens* (and *chrétiennes* which is not even here) being the translation of *christians*.

Finally, some conjugation omissions are observed, for the English word *believe* for instance, the proposed translations are *croyez, croire, croient,* and *crois* but not *croyons* and we later have *believed* with only *croyait* as translation.

All these inconsistencies open important questions about the evaluation process and suggest a careful handcrafted validation which will undoubtedly strengthen the BLI shared task.

6. Conclusion

We presented in this paper the participation of the TALN/LS2N team at the BUCC shared task. We used concatenation of classic embeddings models (character Skipgram and character CBOW) from fastText to get our first results. Graphical proximity of many translation pairs led us to strengthen our system based on a perfect cognates strategy. This latter tend to beat embedding methods on some language pairs. As both methods were effective in different frequency ranges, we combined them to pump up our results on all the language pairs except the two containing Russian. We add that the Wikipedia corpora seem to be more suited for our approach for bilingual lexicon induction than the WaCKy corpora, contradicting the initial claim of the organizers. Finally, we noted and reported multiple problems on the training seed lexicons, the most visible one being the presence of graphically identical pairs on the English-Russian pair, whereas the two languages have a different alphabet. Also, the presence of multiple words not belonging to the language of interest and many proper names, with many of them being graphically identical, making the utility of these pairs questionable. At last, some inconsistencies are present (at least for the French part of these lists) with the inflectional morphology, and with the verb conjugation.

Acknowledgments

We would like to thank the organizers for this exciting challenge. This research has received funding from the French National Research Agency under grant ANR-17-CE23-0001 ADDICTE (Distributional analysis in specialized domain) as well as the Canadian Institute for Data Valorisation (IVADO).

References

Alaux, J., Grave, E., Cuturi, M., and Joulin, A. (2018). Unsupervised hyperalignment for multilingual word embeddings. *CoRR*, abs/1811.01124.

Artetxe, M., Labaka, G., and Agirre, E. (2018a). Generalizing and improving bilingual word embedding mappings with a multi-step framework of linear transformations. In *Proceedings of the Thirty-Second AAAI Conference on Artificial Intelligence*, pages 5012–5019, New Orleans, LA, USA.

Artetxe, M., Labaka, G., and Agirre, E. (2018b). A robust self-learning method for fully unsupervised cross-lingual mappings of word embeddings. In *Proceedings of the 56th Annual Meeting of the Association for Computational Linguistics (ACL'18)*, pages 789–798, Melbourne, Australia.

Baroni, M., Bernardini, S., Ferraresi, A., and Zanchetta, E. (2009). The wacky wide web: a collection of very large linguistically processed web-crawled corpora. *Language resources and evaluation*, 43(3):209–226.

Bojanowski, P., Grave, E., Joulin, A., and Mikolov, T. (2016). Enriching word vectors with subword information. *CoRR*, abs/1607.04606.

Chen, X. and Cardie, C. (2018). Unsupervised multilingual word embeddings. In *Proceedings of the 2018 Conference on Empirical Methods in Natural Language Processing*, pages 261–270, Brussels, Belgium.

Conneau, A., Lample, G., Ranzato, M., Denoyer, L., and Jégou, H. (2017). Word translation without parallel data. *CoRR*, abs/1710.04087.

Grave, E., Bojanowski, P., Gupta, P., Joulin, A., and Mikolov, T. (2018). Learning word vectors for 157 languages. In *Proceedings of the International Conference on Language Resources and Evaluation (LREC'18)*, Miyazaki, Japan.

Hazem, A. and Morin, E. (2018). Leveraging meta-embeddings for bilingual lexicon extraction from specialized comparable corpora. In *Proceedings of the 27th International Conference on Computational Linguistics*, pages 937–949. Association for Computational Linguistics.

Mikolov, T., Sutskever, I., Chen, K., Corrado, G. S., and Dean, J. (2013). Distributed representations of words and phrases and their compositionality. In C. J. C. Burges, et al., editors, *Advances in Neural Information Processing Systems 26*, pages 3111–3119. Curran Associates, Inc.

Pennington, J., Socher, R., and Manning, C. (2014). Glove: Global vectors for word representation. In *Proceedings of the 2014 Conference on Empirical Methods in Natural Language Processing (EMNLP)*, pages 1532–1543, Doha, Qatar.

Smith, S. L., Turban, D. H. P., Hamblin, S., and Hammerla, N. Y. (2017). Offline bilingual word vectors, orthogonal transformations and the inverted softmax. *CoRR*, abs/1702.03859.

Taitelbaum, H., Chechik, G., and Goldberger, J. (2019a). A multi-pairwise extension of Procrustes analysis for multilingual word translation. In *Proceedings of the 2019 Conference on Empirical Methods in Natural Language Processing and the 9th International Joint Conference on Natural Language Processing (EMNLP-IJCNLP'19)*, pages 3560–3565, Hong Kong, China.

Taitelbaum, H., Chechik, G., and Goldberger, J. (2019b). Multilingual word translation using auxiliary languages. In *Proceedings of the 2019 Conference on Empirical Methods in Natural Language Processing and the 9th International Joint Conference on Natural Language Processing (EMNLP-IJCNLP'19)*, pages 1330–1335, Hong Kong, China.

Wada, T., Iwata, T., and Matsumoto, Y. (2019). Unsupervised multilingual word embedding with limited resources using neural language models. In *Proceedings of the 57th Annual Meeting of the Association for Computational Linguistics (ACL'19)*, pages 3113–3124, Florence, Italy.

Xing, C., Wang, D., Liu, C., and Lin, Y. (2015). Normalized word embedding and orthogonal transform for bilingual word translation. In *Proceedings of the 2015 Conference of the North American Chapter of the Association for Computational Linguistics: Human Language Technologies (NAACL-HLT'15)*, pages 1006–1011, Denver, CO, USA.

Proceedings of the 13th Workshop on Building and Using Comparable Corpora, pages 61–64
Language Resources and Evaluation Conference (LREC 2020), Marseille, 11–16 May 2020

cEnTam: Creation and Validation of a New English-Tamil Bilingual Corpus

Sanjanasri JP, Premjith B, Vijay Krishna Menon, Soman K P
Center for Computational Engineering and Networking (CEN), Amrita School of Engineering,
Amrita Vishwa Vidyapeetham, Coimbatore- 641112, India
{p_sanjanashree, b_premjith, m_vijaykrishna}@cb.amrita.edu, kp_soman@amrita.edu

Abstract

Natural Language Processing (NLP), is the field of artificial intelligence that gives the computer the ability to interpret, perceive and extract appropriate information from human languages. Contemporary NLP is predominantly a data-driven process. It employs machine learning and statistical algorithms to learn language structures from textual corpus. While applications of NLP in English, certain European languages such as Spanish, German, etc. have been tremendous, it is not so, in many Indian languages. There are obvious advantages in creating aligned bilingual and multilingual corpora. Machine translation, cross-lingual information retrieval, content availability and linguistic comparison are a few of the most sought after applications of such parallel corpora. This paper explains and validates a parallel corpus we created for English-Tamil bilingual pair.

1. Introduction

Accurately analyzing NLP tasks requires good quality corpus. However, creating such a corpus is a tedious and laborious task. There are only a few open-source bilingual corpora available for English-Tamil language pair. Existing corpora for English-Tamil language pair is listed in Table 1. EnTam (EnTam-v2) (Ramasamy et al., 2014) is an English-Tamil bilingual corpus crawled from the publicly available websites, especially form cinema, general news domain, and bible data. The author of this paper claimed that the corpus is plain raw data and requires some pre-processing before handling it for any NLP applications. Open subtitles (Lison and Tiedemann, 2016) is the corpus collected from the opus website. This corpus comprises bilingual movie subtitles that belong to the spoken language category. Tanzil (Tiedemann, 2012) is a collection of Quran translations compiled by the Tanzil project. OPUS website (Tiedemann, 2012) is a collection of English-Tamil bilingual localization files from open-source software projects like Ubuntu, KDE4, and GNOME. QED (QCRI Educational Domain) corpus (Abdelali et al., 2014) is again a data set belonging to the spoken language category. It includes bilingual subtitles of educational videos and lectures. The bilingual corpus is transcribed and translated using the AMARA web-based platform.

The following shortcomings were observed based on the information from these existing bilingual corpora:

- **Tanzil** is mostly translated poetry and **Bible** is non-contemporary prose. Hence, this cannot be utilised for generic NLP applications; specific dictionary has to be created.

- **EnTam** is a raw unstructured web corpus and contains a lot of noisy tokens such as image hyperlinks and other non-text web content. High-end pre-processing is required to make it usable. The sentences are aligned merely based on delimiter. The website data is crawled and is roughly comparable, which adversely effects bilingual embedding algorithms due to its high noise content.

- **Open subtitles** and **QED** are corpora belonging to

spoken language style category, which might not help in efficient textual analysis.

- **Tatoeba** corpus has a minimal number of parallel sentences. Hence, it could not be used as standalone data for training machine learning models.

Although these existing corpora for English-Tamil language pair may still be useful in certain bilingual applications, we believe that these corpora still lack features that are strongly desirable for their use in word embedding context. Therefore, for justifiable analysis of semantic relatedness between language pairs using word embedding, a standard corpus has to be developed.

2. Data

Years back, creating bilingual corpus was an uphill task in NLP especially for Indian languages. Internet breaks the language barrier for both content and access today. Many literary works such as novels, short stories, plays, etc. are being translated among various languages and are made easily accessible mostly through crowd-sourcing. Having rich literature in a language doesn't imply that it is resource rich, at least in a bilingual context; creating parallel corpus is still a mammoth effort. The data provided is a collection of sentences taken from textbooks, bilingual novels, story books and bilingual websites that includes tourism, health and news domain. The source data are merely comparable. The sample data is shown in Table 2.

3. Experimental design

The methodology for acquisition of parallel corpus (cEnTam) from printed books and websites is shown in Fig. 1 and 2. In the pre-processing phase, the scanned images are cropped, skewed, rotated and even re-scanned wherever necessary to remove noise. The cleaned image is converted to text using Google OCR API. The text is further cleansed manually. It was necessary to ensure that the lines do not get blended with each other or that the font interferes with character recognition. The characters were at times not detected properly, which had to be typed manually.

Table 1: Details of existing corpora for English-Tamil language pair

Source	Domain	Sentences	English Tokens	Tamil Tokens
EnTam	Generic (bible, cinema, news)	169.8k	3.9M	2.7M
Open subtitles	Movie Subtitles	32.4k	0.2M	0.2M
OPUS website	Ubuntu,KDE4, GNOME	111.1k	3.2M	1.0M
Tateoba	Simple Sentences	0.3k	2.1k	1.6k
Tanzil	Quran Data	93.5k	2.8M	7.0M
QED	Subtitles of Educational Videos	0.7k	1.0M	0.5M

Table 2: Sample data for cEnTam

English	Tamil
kerala express connects daily to delhi	*thinamum kaeraLa viraivu rayil thilliyOtu inNaikkiRathu*
i was at the cinema yesterday	*Naan NaeRRu thirai aranGkaththil iruNthaen*
thambidurai unanimously elected to lok sabha deputy speaker	*makkaLavai thunNai chapaaNaayakaraaka athimukavil thampithurai orumanathaaka thaervu cheyyappattaar*
this medicine will protect children from fever	*iNtha maruNthu kuzhaNthaikaLai kaaychchalil iruNthu kaakkum)*

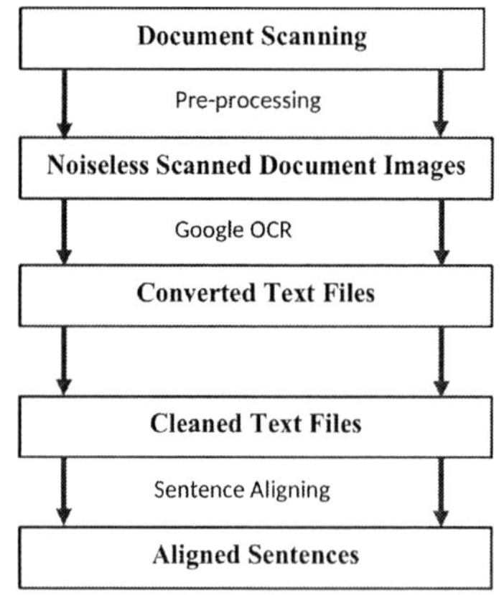

Figure 1: Block diagram for creation of parallel corpus (cEnTam) - printed books

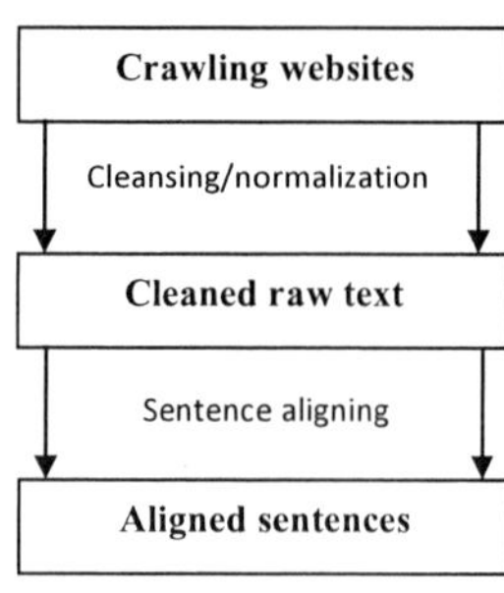

Figure 2: Block diagram for creation of parallel corpus (cEnTam) - website data

Table 3: Details of cEnTam Corpus.

Corpus Type	English (#. of sentences)	Tamil (#. of sentences)
Monolingual	457396	563568
Bilingual	56495	56495

In case of website data, the selective bilingual/monolingual websites are crawled using python library *"Scrapy"* to extract the main text from the web pages. Headline, hyperlinks, images, name(s) of author(s), publication date are all ignored. The extracted raw text is cleansed and normalized to remove punctuation, quotations, brackets, currency chars and digits. Since bilingual websites are already parallel, the sentences are aligned based on delimiter. Aligned sentences are checked manually for corrections. Lengthy sentences are split into shorter ones, to maintain consistency in data. The shorter sentence (less than six tokens/sentence) are less likely to contain any of the linguistic rule patterns, hence, the sentences vary from six to thirty tokens in length, with a corpus average of fifteen tokens per sentence including functional words. . Please find the specifics about the corpus in Table 3.

4.   Comparative Analysis of corpora

The bilingual corpora are assessed based on *coherence*. In a coherent text, there are logical links between the words, sentences, and paragraphs of the text. Coherence can be quantified by measuring similarity between sentences and/or documents. We use simple cosine similarity measure using appropriate embeddings, called the neighbourhood method. This approach assesses the translation quality of words using the bilingual embeddings trained on the aforementioned corpora. It measures the accuracy of the translation for the given source word. The evaluation is based on a test dictionary (AI, 2020).

For computing coherence between the sentences, we need to use pre-trained monolingual embeddings in English and Tamil separately from each corpora (Table 1). Using MUSE (Conneau et al., 2017), we can generate bilingual embeddings of all the pairs of words in the vocabulary, in an unsupervised manner. We then use these bilingual word embeddings to generate bilingual sentence embeddings. This embeds sentences of source and target language in a shared vector space. Average cosine similarity of the sentences is used as an accuracy metric.

5.   Neural Machine Translation

This section discusses the comparative study of various corpora, using Neural Machine Translation (NMT) using the corpus created in-house (cEnTam) and EnTam. The process of translating lots of sentences is very complex and we chose to do it only on two main data sets. The quality of translation is directly assessed using a BLEU and RIBES scoring.A simple NMT architecture is used, to keep the training easy and fast which is shown in Fig. 3. The induced translation is evaluated based on both Bilingual Evaluation Understudy (BLEU) (Papineni et al., 2002) and Rank-based Intuitive Bilingual Evaluation Score (RIBES) (Isozaki et al., 2010) metric. However, BLEU is known to be a standard metric for Machine Translation (MT) evaluation, RIBES is best suited for distant pair languages like English and Tamil (Tan et al., 2015). The accuracy can be improved further when used with attention mechanism (Bahdanau et al., 2014). This evaluation can demonstrate the better coherence of our Corpus.

6.   Results

Efficacy of the bilingual embeddings trained over the various corpora are assessed using word level and sentence level neighbourhood. This method is inspired from (Mikolov et al., 2013). In this approach, we test whether the bilingual embedding is able to generate an appropriate target word for the given source word within the confining window of top similar words. Table 4 shows the performance of Nearest Neighbourhood word tasks.

The percentage accuracy of how likely the target words appear as nearest neighbour to the source word within K (words) window size, is measured. We see the value for K=1 itself is very high for our corpus compared to other corpora. This proves that the parallel sentences in our corpus are more coherent compared to others. Table 5 shows the performance of sentence similarity task on various corpora. Considering the performance of the all other corpora in the aforementioned tasks, cEnTam shows considerably better results; EnTam shows the next best results. Henceforth, for comparative study using NMT, cEnTam and EnTam corpora were used. The results are shown in

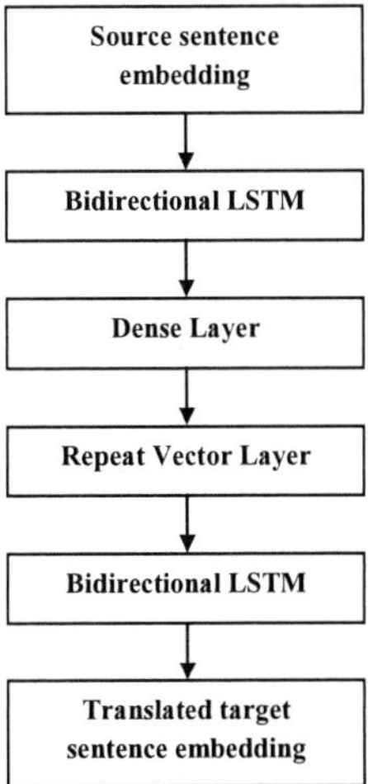

Figure 3: Neural Machine Translation Deep network used for testing corpora performances.

Table 4: Accuracy of the Nearest Neighbour analysis of word translation task using various window sizes in different corpora. The value represents the relative frequency of finding the target translation for a source word amongst the paired sentences expressed

Corpora	Window size (Number of target words / 100 source words)		
	K=1	K=5	K=10
EnTam	11.83	18.58	21.7
Open subtitles	11.61	18.37	20.53
OPUS website	4.91	7.06	7.8
Tanzil	0.47	0.95	1.05
QED	0.06	0.13	0.15
cEnTam	*27.08*	*35.15*	*39.36*

Table 6. Both the BLEU and RIBES metric yield better scores over translations created using cEnTam corpus over EnTam. This further proves the quality of cEnTam over EnTam in a real machine translation system.

Table 5: Average cosine sentence similarity of various corpora. A highest average and a lower deviation of cosine relations between sentence indicate coherence of the corpus.

Corpora	Avg. Cosine Similarity	Std.Dev
EnTam	0.12	0.09
Open subtitles	0.06	0.07
OPUS website	0.07	0.10
Tanzil	0.03	0.13
QED	0.04	0.21
cEnTam	*0.32*	*0.04*

Table 6: Results of Neural Machine Translation system performance with EnTam and cEnTam corpora

Corpora	BLEU	RIBES
EnTam	0.12	0.52
cEnTam	*0.39*	*0.74*

7. Conclusion

Non-existence of standard bilingual corpora is a major obstruction in effectively utilizing NLP technologies in many languages. Whether it is explainable (AI) analysis of semantic relatedness between language pairs or end-to-end deep learning models, it is necessary to have a standard bilingual corpus. Here, we have effectively demonstrated and implemented a methodology to create bilingual corpora, those are comparatively fast and requires less human effort. The corpus created is sentence aligned, hence it can be used for implementing NLP applications such as machine translation, cross-lingual information retrieval, semantic comparison and bilingual dictionary induction. The validations using nearest neighbourhood approach, sentence similarity and neural machine translation.

Acknowledgement

We would like to thank Dr.Rajendran S, Professor & Head (Retd.), Department of Linguistics, Tamil University, Thanjavur, India currently serving as adjunct professor in Centre for Computational Engineering and Networking (CEN), Amrita University, India, Dr. A.G. Menon, associate professor (Retd.), Department of Indian Studies and Department of Comparative Linguistics, Leiden University and Dr. Loganathan Ramaswamy, Machine Learning Engineer at MSD and main author of EnTam corpus, Prague, Czech Republic for their immense suggestion on creating bilingual corpus.

Bibliographical References

Abdelali, A., Guzman, F., Sajjad, H., and Vogel, S. (2014). The AMARA corpus: Building parallel language resources for the educational domain. In *Proceedings of the Ninth International Conference on Language Resources and Evaluation (LREC'14)*, pages 1856–1862, Reykjavik, Iceland, May. European Language Resources Association (ELRA).

AI, F. (2016). Pretrained vectors fasttext. https://fasttext.cc/docs/en/pretrained-vectors.html.

AI, F. (2020). Tamil-english dictionary. https://dl.fbaipublicfiles.com/arrival/dictionaries/ta-en.txt, April.

Bahdanau, D., Cho, K., and Bengio, Y. (2014). Neural machine translation by jointly learning to align and translate.

Conneau, A., Lample, G., Ranzato, M., Denoyer, L., and Jégou, H. (2017). Word translation without parallel data. *arXiv preprint arXiv:1710.04087*.

Gouws, S., Bengio, Y., and Corrado, G. (2015). Bilbowa: Fast bilingual distributed representations without word alignments. In *ICML*, volume 37 of *JMLR Workshop and Conference Proceedings*, pages 748–756.

Isozaki, H., Hirao, T., Duh, K., Sudoh, K., and Tsukada, H. (2010). Automatic evaluation of translation quality for distant language pairs. In *Proceedings of the 2010 Conference on Empirical Methods in Natural Language Processing*, pages 944–952, Cambridge, MA, October. Association for Computational Linguistics.

Lison, P. and Tiedemann, J. (2016). OpenSubtitles2016: Extracting large parallel corpora from movie and TV subtitles. In *Proceedings of the Tenth International Conference on Language Resources and Evaluation (LREC'16)*, pages 923–929, Portorož, Slovenia, May. European Language Resources Association (ELRA).

Mikolov, T., Le, Q. V., and Sutskever, I. (2013). Exploiting similarities among languages for machine translation. *CoRR*, abs/1309.4168.

Papineni, K., Roukos, S., Ward, T., and Zhu, W.-J. (2002). Bleu: a method for automatic evaluation of machine translation. In *Proceedings of the 40th Annual Meeting of the Association for Computational Linguistics*, pages 311–318, Philadelphia, Pennsylvania, USA, July. Association for Computational Linguistics.

Ramasamy, L., Bojar, O., and Žabokrtský, Z. (2014). EnTam: An english-tamil parallel corpus (EnTam v2.0). LINDAT/CLARIN digital library at the Institute of Formal and Applied Linguistics (ÚFAL), Faculty of Mathematics and Physics, Charles University.

Tan, L. L., Dehdari, J., and van Genabith, J. (2015). An awkward disparity between bleu / ribes scores and human judgements in machine translation. In *Proceedings of the Workshop on Asian Translation (WAT-2015)*, pages 74–81. Association for Computational Linguistics.

Tiedemann, J. (2012). Parallel data, tools and interfaces in OPUS. In *Proceedings of the Eighth International Conference on Language Resources and Evaluation (LREC'12)*, pages 2214–2218, Istanbul, Turkey, May. European Language Resources Association (ELRA).

Proceedings of the 13th Workshop on Building and Using Comparable Corpora, pages 65–68
Language Resources and Evaluation Conference (LREC 2020), Marseille, 11–16 May 2020

BUCC2020: Bilingual Dictionary Induction using Cross-lingual Embedding

Sanjanasri JP, Vijay Krishna Menon, Soman K P

Center for Computational Engineering and Networking (CEN), Amrita School of Engineering,
Amrita Vishwa Vidyapeetham, Coimbatore- 641112, India
{p_sanjanashree, m_vijaykrishna}@cb.amrita.edu, kp_soman@amrita.edu

Abstract

This paper presents a deep learning system for the BUCC 2020 shared task: Bilingual dictionary induction from comparable corpora. We have submitted two runs for this shared Task, German (de) and English (en) language pair for "closed track" and Tamil (ta) and English (en) for the "open track". Our core approach focuses on quantifying the semantics of the language pairs, so that semantics of two different language pairs can be compared or transfer learned. With the advent of word embeddings, it is possible to quantify this. In this paper, we propose a deep learning approach which makes use of the supplied training data, to generate cross-lingual embedding. This is later used for inducting bilingual dictionaries from comparable corpora.

1. Introduction

In machine translation, the extraction of bilingual dictionaries from parallel corpora have been conducted very successfully. Theoretically, it is possible to extract multilingual lexical knowledge from comparable rather than from parallel corpora as the former is more abundant than the latter. To implement any machine learning tasks in Natural Language processing (NLP), it is necessary to quantify the semantics (meaning) of the word in a language. Representation of semantics of a word quantitatively is made possible with the evolution of word embeddings (Mikolov et al., 2013a);they are dense distributed vector representations of words. This numerical representation mimics the linguistic phenomena such as lexical, syntactic, morphological and other complex phenomena such as ambiguity, negation, lemmas, inference and so on. Contemporary vector training algorithms such as GloVe and Word2Vec (Pennington et al., 2014; Mikolov et al., 2013c) are more accurate in capturing word to word semantics than conventional vector space models such as Latent Semantic Analysis (LSA) (Deerwester et al., 1990) and perform better in almost all downstream tasks in NLP (Treviso et al., 2017; Bansal et al., 2014; Guo et al., 2014).

In this paper, we train a transfer learning model/Deep Neural Network(DNN) using pre-trained monolingual embeddings of the given bilingual dictionary. Source embedding is given to DNN, so it generates a target embedding. The generated embedding is compared with the original (monolingual) embedding to find the closest embedding. The word corresponding to the closest embedding is identified as the word translation of the given source word. Simply, we perform a reverse look up to identify the correct word translation from the original embedding given the transfer learned embedding.

Section 2 describes the systems that are experimented for this task. Section 3 gives the details of the data used for this experimentation. Section 4 gives insight about the computational complexity. Section 5 details the evaluation method carried out to justify the system. Section 6 gives the results of the systems. Section 7 gives some concluding inferences and remarks.

2. System Description

The main objective of this work is to develop an efficient and accurate transfer learning method for attaining *'cross-lingual'* word embeddings without the large monolingual and bilingual corpus. The system was developed in four stages; each improving the accuracy. The test data result submitted is run on the system that gave us the best accuracy. System one derives the translation matrix for the language pair using the standard method (direct linear mapping) (Mikolov et al., 2013b). Given pairs of word vectors in a source and target language $< x_i, y_i >_{i=1}^{n}$ respectively, we calculate the transformation matrix (W) between the two languages utilizing pseudo inverse $X^+ = (X^T X)^{-1} X^T$, as follows:

$$XW = Y$$
$$W = X^+ Y \tag{1}$$

System two and three deploy deep learning network to learn the mapping between two different language embeddings. In this method we train a transfer learning model to generate cross-lingual embedding. Our method has obvious advantages over the bilingual embedding (Chandar et al., 2014; Gouws et al., 2015), because bilingual embeddings might compromise semantics in order to project each language (source and target) into the common vector space; the semantic properties pertaining to the language might be lost as the model considers only the common semantic features between the languages. Our method generates cross-lingual embedding by projecting the vectors of one language into another language space without compromising the actual semantics of both the languages. Also, to train an efficient bilingual embedding, it is necessary to have large bilingual resources. The transfer learning model can generate better cross-lingual embedding when trained with as minimum as 5000 dictionary words. System two is implemented on a Multi Layer Perceptron (MLP) and system three uses Convolutional Neural Networks (CNN).

System four is a mere extension of the CNN with a small topical modification. It fine tunes the pre-trained translational model (system 3) using neighbourhood relationships. The systems of each language pair are implemented

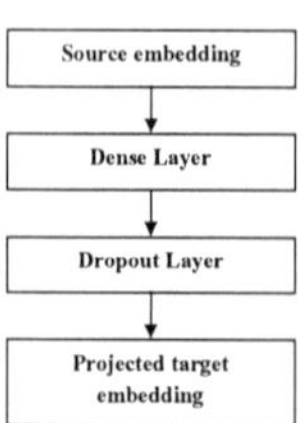

Figure 1: Architecture of MLP for learning the transfer model for cross-lingual embedding

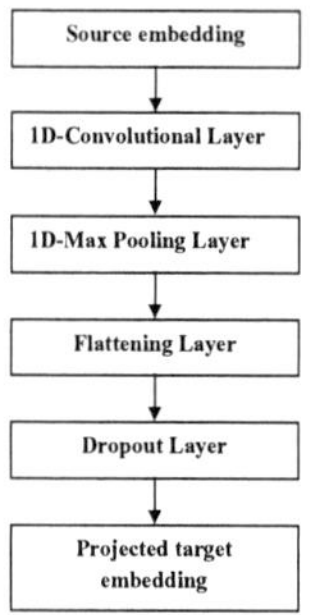

Figure 2: Architecture of CNN for learning the transfer model for cross-lingual embedding

as mentioned above, they are further trained over the mono-lingual embedding of bilingual word pairs of the respective languages.

2.1. Multi Layer Perceptron

The multi layer perceptrons (MLP) is a fully connected DNN that holds a special place in NLP for intuitive non-linear modeling. Our MLP topology possesses three dense layers, that uses Rectified Linear Unit (ReLU) as its activation. The dropout layer that follows immediate to every dense layer avoids overfitting in training. Cosine proximity is used as the loss function and RMSprop as optimizer. Figure 1 depicts the architecture of MLP.

2.2. 1D- Convolutional Neural Network

The architecture of CNN has five layers, a CNN layer followed by maxpooling, flatten layer, dropout layer and a dense layer. Rectified Linear Unit (ReLU) is used as activation function in each layer. Again, the cosine proximity and RMSprop is used as loss function and optimizer respectively for training. The CNN architecture is shown in Figure 2.

2.3. Fine-tuned Convolutional Neural Network (Fine-tuned CNN)

In this architecture of CNN, the translation model is trained on neighbourhood relationship of source language word pairs given the cosine similarity between the correspond-

ing target language word pairs as labels. The core objective of this network focuses on fine tuning the previously learned translational model to improve on neighbourhood relations.

For training, embeddings of randomly chosen source language word pairs (wv_{s_i}, wv_{s_j}) from the dictionary is given as an inputs to model1 and model2. The model1 and model2 are identical copies of pre-trained translational model discussed in section 2.2. The outputs of model1 and model2, transfer learned/projected target language word vectors $(wv_{t_i^*}, wv_{t_j^*})$, is passed on to the dot layer, that computes the cosine proximity between the vectors. The cosine distance/output of the dot layer is passed on to dropout layer to avoid over fitting and finally passed on to dense layer, where linear activation is used. For back propagation, the cosine distance between the corresponding target language words (w_{t_i}, w_{t_j}) for the source language word (w_{s_i}, w_{s_j}) is given as labels, mean squared error and RMSprop is used as a loss and optimizer respectively. Please note, that, model1 and model2 are already trained and back propagating with the cosine similarity of the word pairs helps in better learning of the neighbourhood relations. The topology of this model is shown in Figure 3

3. Data

For "closed track", German (de) and English (en) language pairs, we used the FastText pre-trained embeddings of Wacky corpora (Conneau et al., 2017) and the given bilingual dictionary for training. For "open track", Tamil (ta) and English (en) language pairs, FastText pre-trained embeddings of crawled web corpus (Bojanowski et al., 2017; Pre-trained, 2019) and in-house dictionary is used. Details of the dataset used for the tasks is shown in Table 1

4. Computational Complexity

To induce a word translation for the source word, we perform a reverse look up of the transfer learned target vector with the original target monolingual embedding. Given a set of source and target word $< w_{s_i}, w_{t_i} >$ and their corresponding embeddings (original monolingual embeddings) $< wv_{s_i}, wv_{t_i} >$ and transfer learned target embedding$< wv_{t_i^*} >$. For every query source word w_{s_i}, the correct target word w_{t_i} is identified by locating the target embedding wv_{t_i} that is the closest neighbour to the transfer learned/projected target word embedding $wv_{t_i^*}$, where cosine similarity is computed as a measure between the embedding.

However, performing the reverse lookup is computationally intensive. For instance, the embedding size of each test data (German (de) and Tamil(ta)) is $\in \mathbb{R}^{2000 \times 300}$ and English pre-trained Wacky and Crawled web corpus is approximately 2 billion words. Henceforth, the size of original

Table 1: Description of Data

Language Pairs	Train	Test
	(#. of word pairs)	(# of word pairs)
de - en	10095	6000
ta - en	21100	1999

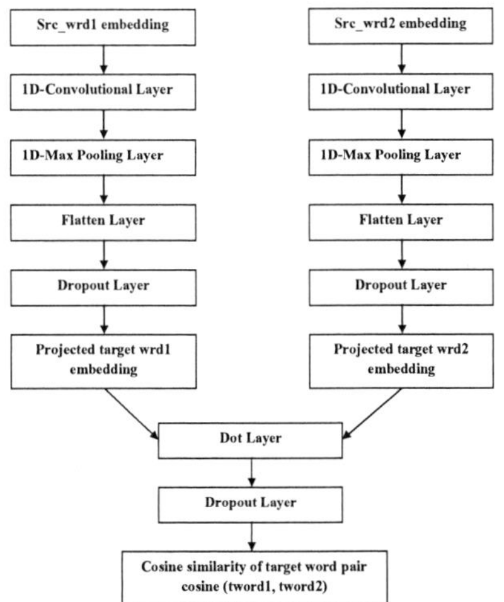

Figure 3: Architecture of CNN for learning the transfer model based on neighbourhood relations for cross-lingual embedding

embedding is $\in \mathbb{R}^{2E9 \times 300}$. The word vectors are of double data type (8 bytes). The cartesian product of the original embedding and transfer learned test embedding would sum upto size of $\in \mathbb{R}^{4E12 \times 300}$ (approximately, four trillion). Computing such huge dataset takes months for a normal computer system to compute. This complex computation is deployed to the cluster using Apache Spark® Framework. The word pairs are filtered based on cosine similarity. The figure 4 shows the architecture.

5. Evaluation Tasks

We know that word embeddings translate semantic relationships to spatial distances, in a good word embedding model the semantically related word pairs in a languages are expected to have closer spatial distance (higher similarity score) in their respective embeddings. We use this linguistic aspect to evaluate our cross-lingual word embeddings. Here, we treat the original (monolingually trained) embedding as our ground truth and compare the global neighbourhood behavior of the generated embeddding. Algorithm 1 explains this. The original (monolingual pretrained) and transfer learned embedding are represented as $OrigVec$ and $TransVec$; N represents the size of the test set. The similarity metric between two words vectors a and b is computed using cosine distance as given in Equation 2.

$$cos(a,b) = \frac{a^T b}{||a|| \cdot ||b||} \quad (2)$$

6. Results

The percentage accuracy of the test data on transfer learned model of each language pairs, German-English (de-en) and Tamil-English (ta-en), tested over various systems is shown

---

Algorithm 1: Algorithm for computing percentage accuracy for global neighbourhood behaviour of the transfer learned embeddings

Input: Input:$OrigVec, TransVec$
Output: Output: $Accuracy$

$\quad k, i \leftarrow 0$
$\quad$**for** $i < N$ **do**
$\quad\quad$**for** $j < N$ **do**
$\quad\quad\quad CosOrigVec[k] =$
$\quad\quad\quad cos(OrigVec[i], OrigVec[j])$
$\quad\quad\quad CosTransVec[k] =$
$\quad\quad\quad cos(TransVec[i], TransVec[j])$
$\quad\quad\quad k = k + 1$
$\quad\quad$**end for**
$\quad$**end for**
$\quad sum, i \leftarrow 0$
$\quad$**for** $i < N * N$ **do**
$\quad\quad grad = CosOrigVec[i] - CosTransVec[i]$
$\quad\quad tmp = grad * grad$
$\quad\quad sum = sum + tmp$
$\quad$**end for**
$\quad RMSE = sqrt(sum/(N * N))$
$\quad PerErr = (RMSE/2) * 100$
$\quad Accuracy = 100 - PerErr$

---

in Table 2. In fine-tuned CNN network (CNN+NN), the dictionary is inducted by passing test data to model1 and the output of model1 is calculated for percentage accuracy on global neighbourhood. From the results in Table 2, it is evident that CNN+NN network outperforms the other three models in each language pair. Henceforth, the final result submitted for the shared task is run on CNN+NN network

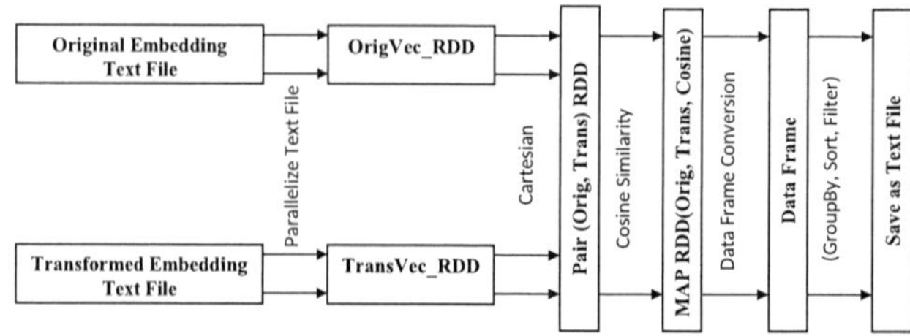

Figure 4: Block diagram for reverse look up of dictionary using Apache Spark® Framework

model.

Table 2: Percentage Accuracy of transfer model of various systems

Models	Language pairs	
	de - en	ta - en
Linear Mapping	73.01	76.05
MLP	80.67	85.52
CNN	85.16	90.33
CNN+NN	*89.91*	*93.65*

7. Conclusion

In this paper, we were able to generate bilingual dictionary for language pairs, German-English (de-en) and Tamil-English (ta-en) by using *'cross-lingual'* embeddings (vectors in separate space, mapped) that is trained on neighbourhood relationship between source language word pairs. As word embedding has no ground truth to evaluate the cross-lingual embedding, we also proposed an evaluation method to validate the model.

For *'de-en'* and *'ta-en'* language pairs, the model is trained with 10095 and 21100 FastText pre-trained monolingual embedding of bilingual words. We started with linear mapping system, as the results were not satisfactory, we moved on to deep learning network. In deep network, CNN gave better accuracy than MLP. Hence, the CNN network was further fine-tuned with a neighbourhood information of source language. This gave the best accuracy among every other systems. Henceforth, test data was run on this system. The core system generates the transfer learned/projected target embedding for the given source embedding. The generated target embedding is compared with the original monolingual target embedding to find the correct target word translation for the source word. To do this reverse lookup process, Apache Spark® Scala language APIs is utilized to manage the computational complexity and speed up.

Bibliographical References

Bansal, M., Gimpel, K., and Livescu, K. (2014). Tailoring continuous word representations for dependency parsing. In *Proceedings of the 52nd Annual Meeting of the Association for Computational Linguistics (Volume 2: Short Papers)*, pages 809–815. Association for Computational Linguistics.

Bojanowski, P., Grave, E., Joulin, A., and Mikolov, T. (2017). Enriching word vectors with subword information. *Transactions of the Association for Computational Linguistics*, 5:135–146.

Chandar, A. P. S., Lauly, S., Larochelle, H., Khapra, M. M., Ravindran, B., Raykar, V. C., and Saha, A. (2014). An autoencoder approach to learning bilingual word representations. *CoRR*, abs/1402.1454.

Conneau, A., Lample, G., Ranzato, M., Denoyer, L., and Jégou, H. (2017). Word translation without parallel data. *CoRR*, abs/1710.04087.

Deerwester, S., Dumais, S. T., Furnas, G. W., Landauer, T. K., and Harshman, R. (1990). Indexing by latent semantic analysis. *JOURNAL OF THE AMERICAN SOCIETY FOR INFORMATION SCIENCE*, 41(6):391–407.

Gouws, S., Bengio, Y., and Corrado, G. (2015). Bilbowa: Fast bilingual distributed representations without word alignments. In *ICML*, volume 37 of *JMLR Workshop and Conference Proceedings*, pages 748–756.

Guo, J., Che, W., Wang, H., and Liu, T. (2014). Revisiting embedding features for simple semi-supervised learning. In *EMNLP*.

Mikolov, T., Chen, K., Corrado, G., and Dean, J. (2013a). Efficient estimation of word representations in vector space. *CoRR*, abs/1301.3781.

Mikolov, T., Le, Q. V., and Sutskever, I. (2013b). Exploiting similarities among languages for machine translation. *CoRR*, abs/1309.4168.

Mikolov, T., Sutskever, I., Chen, K., Corrado, G., and Dean, J. (2013c). Distributed representations of words and phrases and their compositionality. *CoRR*, abs/1310.4546.

Pennington, J., Socher, R., and Manning, C. D. (2014). Glove: Global vectors for word representation. In *EMNLP*, volume 14, pages 1532–1543.

Pre-trained, E. (2019). https://github.com/Kyubyong/wordvectors, June.

Treviso, M. V., Shulby, C. D., and Aluísio, S. M. (2017). Evaluating word embeddings for sentence boundary detection in speech transcripts. *CoRR*, abs/1708.04704.